A *Jane Austen* COMPENDIUM

VIOLET POWELL

A
Jane Austen
COMPENDIUM

The Six Major Novels

Heinemann: London

First published in Great Britain 1993
by William Heinemann Ltd
an imprint of Reed Consumer Books Ltd
Michelin House 81 Fulham Road London SW3 6RB
and Auckland Melbourne Singapore and Toronto

The author has asserted her moral rights

A CIP catalogue record for this book
is available at the British Library
ISBN 0 434 59964 6

Phototypeset by Intype, London
Printed in Great Britain
by Clays Ltd, St Ives PLC

*For Catherine
with love*

Contents

On First Looking into Chapman's Austen

The planet of Doctor R. W. Chapman, in all its brilliance, first swum into my ken during the Second World War. The six major novels of Jane Austen were already firmly rooted in my literary consciousness, but I had not appreciated the depth of analysis which could lead a reader onwards to ever greater enjoyment. *Emma*, as I will mention in its place, was my earliest acquaintance, set as a holiday task of the younger of my two brothers, and read aloud by my mother.

Some years later, the elder of my brothers gave me *Emma* and her five companions, bound in one volume, but it was a month at sea which led me to an intensive, totally absorbed, reading. On a voyage to California, via Panama, my husband, Anthony Powell, and I sailed in the flagship of the Danish Mercantile Marine, ms *Canada*. She was to collect a cargo of bananas in the Republic of Panama, to be unloaded at Los Angeles. Unhappily, she was an early casualty of the Second World War, sunk by a mine in the North Sea when war was only a few weeks old.

For reading on board the ms *Canada*, Anthony, though usually favouring Dostoevsky among the Russians, provided himself with Tolstoy's *War and Peace*. I carried with me the six-in-one Jane Austen, already scarred by a number of house moves. We skirted the grey rocks of the Azores, calling at St Thomas, in the Virgin Islands, Kingston, Jamaica, and the Pacific port of Amuelles. While the tramp of Napoleon's armies, marching towards Moscow, kept Anthony company, I had the Bennets and the Elliots as my travelling companions. There was a friendly feeling in the knowledge that, though Mrs Croft, wife of the Admiral in *Persuasion*, 'had never been in the West Indies', she had sailed in neighbouring waters.

The Second World War was at a particular depth of disaster, when I had the good fortune to meet Doctor Chapman as an editor. Anthony and I were sharing a somewhat unlovely house at Petersham with Anthony Andrewes, Fellow of Pembroke College, Oxford, and his wife Alison, both husbands being in the Intelligence Corps, and stationed at the War Office. Each family had a small child, but when these had been caged in their cots, relief from domestic stress, and war news consistently bad, came by way of Doctor Chapman's edition of Jane Austen's novels. In elaborate questionnaires of plots and characters, Doctor Chapman could always be appealed to as an umpire when answers were disputed.

A year or so after the household at Petersham had dispersed, I found myself once again on the move, flying bombs having driven me from the Darenth

Valley, which was on their main route to London. A friend I had made in Kent, Margaret Behrens, had introduced me to the Mirrlees family, then resident at Shamley Green, a Surrey village, some way south of the possible site of Highbury (*Emma*). T. S. Eliot was a regular visitor at weekends, as a supposed escape from London and its bombs. It could have been a change rather than an escape. The Victorian tensions of the Mirrlees household were not unlike the clashes of personality which drove Florence Nightingale to the edge of nervous collapse.

After dinner at Shamley Green, when Eliot kindly allowed me to share in his private bottle of gin, Hope, an associate member of Bloomsbury, insisted that a guessing game should be played. (Her two test questions on *Emma* I will deal with in their proper place.) Besides Hope, T. S. Eliot and myself, the circle was completed by Mrs Mirrlees and her spinster sister, known to the family as Cocky. Mrs Mirrlees, a powerful matriarch, was afflicted by deafness, while her sister Cocky lived in a state of resentment at not having been sought by a rich husband.

In spite of Hope's enthusiasm, these warring elements slowed the game to walking pace. Eventually, Jane Austen was chosen as the subject to be guessed by Hope. She deduced that the subject was a writer, and asked Eliot which modern writer most resembled this author from the past. Eliot had, I think, begun to nod off, but he opened his eyes and suggested 'Winifred Peck'. The novels of this sister of Ronald Knox were published by Faber and Faber, of which firm Eliot was a distinguished ornament. The parallel with Jane Austen perhaps owned more to Eliot's loyalty as a publisher than considered literary opinion.

The birth of my younger son took place a month earlier than it was expected. There was something of a scramble to get to the nursing home, but I did have the presence of mind to add the six-in-one Jane Austen to the layette and the baby's basket. *Sense and Sensibility* seemed to be a good choice to read during a confinement, Mrs Palmer taking such an encouragingly cheerful view of the situation. The perfidy of Willoughby was revealing itself, when a nurse came in to monitor progress, and expressed amazement at the size of the book which I had chosen as a distraction when in labour.

It was some years after this birth that the Jane Austen Society became a happy part of my life. The Society's archives tell of its heroic foundation in the blackest days of 1940, and of its continuous expansion. As it grew, Doctor Chapman became a vice-president, and Elizabeth Jenkins, author of one of the most perceptive biographies of Jane Austen, became a joint secretary. By 1949 they had been joined by Gerald, 7th Duke of Wellington, as president, an office he held until after his eightieth birthday. (He preferred to say that he had retired because he was between eighty and ninety.)

A tradition grew up that a party should be brought from Stratfield Saye to Chawton for the Annual General Meeting of the Jane Austen Society. Whenever Anthony and I joined this party, the characters of Jane Austen's novels were discussed as friends who had shared our lives, and over whose possible futures we could speculate.

On one of the last occasions, our host expatiated on the charming personality of the younger Charles Musgrove (*Persuasion*) as a warmhearted fellow, cheerfully supporting the burden of a querulous wife.

L. P. Hartley, the novelist, was also, usually, a guest, although his habit of arriving late exasperated Wellington, an obsessively punctual man. We had gone into luncheon, when it was announced that 'Mr Hartley was in the hall'.

Dropping his napkin, the host strode from the room to greet the tardy guest. As he went out, I called after him, 'Remember, you are not Sir Walter Elliot. You are Charles Musgrove.' 'I am General Tilney,' asserted the descendant of the first Duke of Wellington. It would, of course, have been quite possible for this ancestor to have served in the army with the Autocrat of Northanger Abbey.

I began this introduction by telling of the brilliance I found 'on first looking into Chapman's Austen'. My debt to Doctor Chapman throughout the writing of this compendium can best be expressed in the words of the Reverend Ernest Bellamy, in I. Compton-Burnett's *Men and Wives*, which Bellamy applied to Jane Austen herself. 'I am on my knees.'

From many books concerned with Jane Austen, I have derived much pleasure and instruction, but there are two authors to whom I owe particular thanks, my friends Elizabeth Jenkins and the late Marghanita Laski. As ever, I must thank my husband, Anthony Powell, for his constructive assistance.

Violet Powell 1992

Sense and Sensibility

Fish And Game . . .
Whenever They Are In Season

MRS JOHN DASHWOOD

Jane Austen had a vehemently low opinion of the contemporary generation of her mother's cousins, the Leighs of Stoneleigh Abbey. On the death of the Reverend Thomas Leigh, she went so far as to describe him as having died 'the possessor of one of the finest Estates in England & of more worthless Nephews and Nieces than any other private man in the United Kingdom'.

The 'worthless Nephew' who inherited Stoneleigh, James Leigh, was a great-grandfather of Margaret Elizabeth Leigh. She was born in the Abbey on 29 October 1849, and died on 22 May 1945. At Stoneleigh the relationship with Jane Austen was hardly stressed, whether or not they knew of her strictures on the behaviour of that branch of the family. There was, however, one incident in *Sense and Sensibility* with which Margaret Leigh, subsequently wife of the 6th Earl of Jersey, made her own grandchildren familiar by frequent quotation. This was the sequence by which John Dashwood's solemn promise, given at his father's deathbed, that he would take care of his half-sisters, and their mother, is chiselled away by the avarice of Mrs John Dashwood.

In the first rush of emotion following his father's death, John Dashwood decided that he would fulfil his promise by giving £1000 to each of his three half-sisters. This decision caused extreme distress to his wife, *née* Fanny Ferrars. Although herself an heiress, she was determined that not a penny of her husband's money should be alienated from their only child. The dialogue in which £3000 is whittled down to £1500, to an annuity, and finally to nothing, showed Jane Austen's mastery of her medium, even at an early stage in her career as a novelist.

Mrs John Dashwood had a trump card up her sleeve, and played it with precision. Her husband had no answer to her argument that had matters been in his father's power, instead of the Norland estate being entailed on their son, John Dashwood's father would have left everything he could to the daughters of his second marriage. Arguing on these lines, she brought her husband to agree that his promise to his father could easily be fulfilled by presents of fish and game, 'whenever these happened to be in season'.

The situation that so amused Margaret Leigh was originally due to the doting affection felt by the previous bachelor owner of Norland for the infant son of the John Dashwoods. Determined that the estate should be passed down undiminished, and disregarding the tender care of his nephew's second wife and her daughters, old Mr Dashwood had tied matters up so that the early death of his nephew had left the widow and her daughters with scanty means.

Jane Austen was a sympathetic and affectionate aunt to a tribe of nephews and nieces, but she had no illusions about the anarchic behaviour of many small children, and of the charm it could have for an elderly relation. Little Henry Dashwood, noisy, selfish, and up to cunning tricks, might not be fairly blamed for blighting the prospects of his half-aunts, but Jane Austen had no hesitation in painting him as the unlovable child of a mean and grasping mother.

The transfer of Mrs Dashwood and her daughters to a cottage in Devonshire, provided by a kinsman, Sir John Middleton, gave John Dashwood the apparent opportunity to fulfil a residual part of his promise to his father. He had determined that he should, at least, be responsible for the removal of his step-mother's furniture and domestic goods. He was, however, thwarted in his final attempt at keeping his promise. Norland Park, in Sussex, was at such a distance from Barton Cottage, situated four miles from Exeter, that Mrs Dashwood's possessions were sent round by water. Mrs John Dashwood suffered exceedingly on seeing china, plate, and a handsome pianoforte belonging to Marianne, sailing out of her ambience. It was wrong, she felt, that the impoverished Mrs Dashwood 'should have any handsome articles of furniture'.

Although there was relief at escaping from the orbit of the unwelcoming Mrs John Dashwood, the mother of the young ladies had a reluctance at moving far away from Norland. Edward Ferrars, brother of Fanny Dashwood, and Elinor the eldest of the three girls, were showing signs of becoming attached. To Elinor's mother the match seemed so desirable, that she was baffled by Edward's diffidence and Elinor's composure. Elinor refused to gratify her intensely romantic sister Marianne by any display of feeling. When she saw the beginnings of this attachment, Mrs John Dashwood let it be known that her mother, Mrs Ferrars, in whose power was the family fortune, had plans for grand marriages for her sons, Edward, and his younger brother, Robert.

Marianne's farewell to Norland was in her best histrionic romantic manner, but, supported by Elinor's strength of character, she did her best not to find Barton Cottage a too deplorable step down in the world. Mrs Dashwood immediately made plans for improvements, contingent on saving money, something she had never been known to practise. Margaret, the youngest sister, did not display much character, and Jane Austen left her as little more than an outline.

Their landlord, Sir John Middleton, gave the Dashwood family a cordial welcome. He was hearty in all his doings, in contrast to his wife, handsome, elegant and well-bred, but otherwise of a reserved coldness. Jane Austen's observation was of the sharpest when she came to write of temperamentally ill-matched couples. She might be said to savour such situations, and in *Sense and Sensibility* she introduced two married pairs whose incongruity approached the grotesque.

The refined Lady Middleton's sister Charlotte, a jolly bouncing girl, had married a Mr Palmer, who would have been a more suitable husband for Lady Middleton. Mr Palmer had an air of sense and fashion, but little willingness to please or be pleased. The sisters had been heiresses, and their mother, Mrs Jennings, was a well-dowered widow. Some idea of Mrs Jennings' approach to life could be gathered from her son-in-law, Mr Palmer, who, accused by his wife of contradicting everybody, replied that he did not know he was contradicting anybody in calling her mother ill-bred.

A symptom of Mrs Jennings' ill-breeding was her habit of teasing young ladies about their supposed admirers. She soon had some excellent material on which to exercise her raillery, owing to an accident to Marianne. With her natural impetuosity, she was running down a steep Devonshire hill, when she fell, and was unable to walk from a badly twisted ankle. Whereupon a gentleman, who was out shooting, gathered Marianne up in his arms, and carried her into her mother's house. This was Marianne's introduction to John Willoughby, the first, but not the least seductive, of Jane Austen's cads.

The immediate attraction between Marianne and Willoughby soon became so obvious that Mrs Jennings had plenty of occasion for her sallies, and she soon had ammunition for testing her wit on Elinor. An indiscreet remark of the youngest sister, Margaret, gave Mrs Jennings the knowledge that Elinor had a liking for a young man whose name began with F. When Edward Ferrars arrived to stay at Barton Cottage, Mrs Jennings at once made the connection, and the unfortunate Elinor was exposed to teasing for a love affair which seemed to be stationary, if not retrogressive.

In the meantime the behaviour of Marianne and Willoughby passed what Elinor considered to be the bounds of decorum. She tried, vainly, to persuade her mother that Marianne's youth would make it prudent to inquire if there was an actual engagement. Mrs Dashwood's romantic delicacy caused her to shun such an interrogation as insulting to the young couple. Jane Austen's description of Marianne's beauty might recall a phrase of F. Scott Fitzgerald, when writing of another seventeen-year-old. 'She was perfect, but the dew was still on her.' Marianne had a glowing complexion with dark eyes and hair. She was, in fact, a beautiful brunette, as Jane Austen's principal heroines tended to be. It would, perhaps, be going too far to say that Jane Austen equated fair hair and blue eyes with mental dimness, but she certainly thought that hazel eyes belonged to bright wits.

L. P. Hartley, in an address to the Jane Austen Society, described Marianne Dashwood as a tragic figure, and, in the novel her potential for tragedy was early recognised by Colonel Brandon, *ami de la maison* of the Middleton family. He was, himself, early marked down as an admirer of Marianne by Mrs Jennings. The first crisis in the novel boiled up when Colonel Brandon left Barton Park for London, without explanation. In an aside to Elinor, Mrs Jennings surmised that he had some business connected with a Miss Williams. Mrs Jennings took distinct pleasure in explaining that this was the Colonel's natural daughter.

Marianne and Willoughby had often laughed at the middle-aged staidness of Colonel Brandon, suggesting that an old age of flannel waistcoats was the best to which he could look forward. Marianne's laughter changed to tears, only a week after the Colonel had left. Willoughby announced that his rich cousin, Mrs Smith, to whom he was the hopeful heir, had precipitately sent him to London on business. Willoughby's farewells were gloomy, and he held out no hope of a speedy return. Marianne wept copiously, but her mother still refused to inquire as to whether there was an engagement.

It was at this uncomfortable moment that Edward

Ferrars arrived. Although his visit pleased the family at Barton Cottage, it did not provide much cheerfulness. At his best, Edward Ferrars was far from lively, his lack of sparkle almost amounting to caricature. Jane Austen was probably correct, psychologically speaking, that his muted nature might have appeal for the composed good sense of Elinor Dashwood. To the experienced reader of novels it would have been immediately apparent that Willoughby with his abundant charm would prove to be unreliable, a potentially vile seducer. The subtle surprise of the plot came when Edward was shown to be, not a seducer, but a man who could conceal an amorous entanglement, while passing as an unattached bachelor.

Hair was considered to have a particular sentimental value in the nineteenth century. Whole scenes of mourning could even be constructed from the hair of a deceased, augmented by that of kindred and friends. Jane Austen used this predeliction twice as an instrument in the plot of *Sense and Sensibility*. Although Margaret Dashwood was not fully developed as a character, she was something of an *enfant terrible*, reporting that she had seen Willoughby begging for, and being given a lock of Marianne's hair.

As she said herself, Marianne was driven mad by the apathetic manner in which Edward conducted his supposed courtship of Elinor. She did however notice that Edward was wearing a ring which held a small plait of hair. Pressed by Marianne, Edward agreed that it was a present from his sister Fanny, and, as it turned out mendaciously, explained that the setting made the hair darker than might be expected. Marianne privately assumed that the ring was a love token from her sister. While Elinor, knowing this to be impossible, cheered her heart by thinking that Edward had without her knowledge, performed a rape of a lock.

The next threat to Elinor's happiness came from the relentless hospitality of Sir John Middleton. Visiting Exeter Mrs Jennings discovered two cousins of her own, Anne and Lucy Steele. Sir John's immediate reaction was to invite the Misses Steele to stay at Barton Park. The prospect of their visit was displeasing to Lady Middleton, whose liking for elegant simplicity was continually hampered by the ebullience of her husband and her mother. Jane Austen gave one of her more sardonic views of the married state by explaining that 'Lady Middleton resigned herself to the idea of [the Misses Steele's visit] with all the philosophy of a well-bred woman, contenting herself with merely giving her husband a gentle reprimand on the subject five or six times a day.'

Apart from her cultivation of the elegant life, Lady Middleton's preoccupation was the spoiling of her children, a singularly unpleasant quartette. The Misses Steele quickly saw the way to ingratiate themselves, and by unstinted praise, and cheerful bearing of childish bullying, established themselves as agreeable guests. Anne, the elder sister, was an ageing young lady, liking to be teased about imaginary admirers, but Lucy, the younger, had a more formidable character. A natural adventuress, Lucy made the most of her pretty features and sharp wits. At first Elinor found Lucy enjoyable company, but soon began to feel that there was something sinister in Lucy's personality. Elinor was also rather disconcerted by the unexpected knowledge of Norland and the Ferrars family displayed by the Misses Steele.

Although Elinor had last seen Edward in a depressed mood, she had not lost confidence in his affection for herself. She made allowances for his lack of occupation, which made him all too dependent on the whims of his tyrannical mother, and for the diffidence which impeded his sluggish courtship. Elinor's characteristic was good sense, but her affection must have clouded her judgement. Her composure was shortly put to the severest test from a totally unexpected quarter.

Besides showing unexpected knowledge of the Dashwoods' background, Lucy Steele also made inquiries about the character of Mrs Ferrars. Elinor parried these from lack of personal acquaintance, and suppressed her own view of the unpleasantness of Edward's mother. Then Lucy threw her bombshell. She was particularly concerned to know the facts of Mrs Ferrars' disposition, because, Lucy simpered, there might come a time when she would be intimately connected with this formidable lady. This would certainly mean that Lucy had the expectation of becoming daughter-in-law to Mrs Ferrars, and Elinor could only assume that Lucy was privately engaged to Edward's brother, Robert.

Elinor felt little pleasure at the idea of Lucy as a sister-in-law, but she was then dealt a *coup de grâce*.

It was four years, Lucy told Elinor, that she had been secretly engaged to Mr Edward Ferrars. Before he went up to Oxford, Edward's education had been entrusted to a Mr Pratt, uncle of the Misses Steele. Presumably Mr Pratt was a classical tutor, but the situation of a young man becoming entangled with a girl in his tutor's family was also classical. This can have been of little consolation to Elinor, who had to face that, a laggard in love, Edward had also been a double-dealer. His only defence can have been that, no favourite at home, he had found a family circle where an attractive girl was prepared to appreciate him. Lucy, for her part, was ready to gamble on Edward's future as the son of a wealthy mother.

At first Elinor clung to the hope that Lucy was building a slight acquaintance with her uncle's pupil into an engagement to marry, a hope soon squashed by Lucy. Not only did she produce Edward's portrait and a recent letter, but she asked Elinor if she had noticed that Edward had been wearing a ring in which Lucy's hair was set. This must have been an additional blow to Elinor, in recollecting that Edward had lied in insisting, against the evidence, that the hair was that of his sister Fanny. Lucy made a point of emphasising that Edward's regard for Elinor and Marianne was that of an affectionate brother. Elinor had no difficulty in reading this as notice to 'keep off the grass', Lucy having scented a rival.

To conceal Lucy's confidences from her mother and Marianne became a main object for Elinor. She felt that she would only suffer more if she had to listen to their inevitable condemnation of Edward. Elinor was, however, no coward soul, and under cover of helping Lucy make a filigree basket for spoilt little Annamaria Middleton, she broached the subject of Lucy's engagement. The verbal duel that followed gained piquancy from the formal language in which it was conducted. Elinor parried Lucy's attempts to get under her guard, which were accompanied by assurances of Edward's unfaltering devotion to his betrothed.

Lucy also declared that, had Edward been attracted to another, the strength of her own devotion would, inevitably, have led her to suspect such a deviation. Neither girl was taken in by this nonsense. Lucy proceeded to probe deeper by declaring that, did Elinor so advise, she would break off her unpromising engagement. Elinor did not fall into this trap, and the duel ended with honours even.

Among Elinor's problems, in her efforts to control the wayward sensibility of her sister, was the difficulty of persuading Marianne to moderate her behaviour when in company with the family at Barton Park. In particular, the earthy tone of Mrs Jennings' conversation had grated on Marianne's nerves to such an extent that Elinor had a struggle to persuade her sister to behave with 'tolerable politeness' towards the jocular old lady.

Marianne's uncivil attitude suddenly changed when Mrs Jennings invited the Misses Dashwood to travel to London with her, and to stay there as her guests. Attempts by Elinor to refuse an invitation from such an unrefined hostess were thwarted by Marianne's eagerness to accept, and Mrs Dashwood's wish that her daughters should widen their knowledge of society. Finding that Marianne was fixed on going to London, even as the guest of Mrs Jennings, Elinor decided that it was her duty to go too. Her purpose was not only to protect her sister, obviously going in pursuit of Willoughby, but also to ensure that kind Mrs Jennings was not left at the mercy of Marianne's whims for companionship.

When installed in the house of Mrs Jennings, near Portman Square and so probably in Upper or Lower Berkeley Street, Marianne immediately wrote to Willoughby. No reply came, and Elinor's heart sank. Finally, after a miserable confrontation at an evening party, Willoughby did reply to Marianne's pathetic request that, had his feelings changed, he should return her letters and the lock of her hair which he possessed. Willoughby's reply was a masterpiece of insolence. He apologised, in patronising terms, for any misapprehension about his feelings towards Marianne. Such feelings, he wrote, would be agreed to be impossible, as he had long been engaged elsewhere. The marriage, he indicated, would take place in a matter of weeks.

When Mrs Jennings heard of Marianne's cruel disappointment, she had recourse to a practical treatment. When her late husband had suffered from cholicky gout nothing did him so much good as a glass of 'the finest old Constantia wine', of which his widow still possessed a quantity. Mrs Jennings poured out a glass for Marianne, on the principle that such a draught from the Cape of Good Hope would be equally effective for a 'disappointed heart'. To avert further distress to Marianne, Elinor asked leave to drink the wine herself, reflecting that her heart was, if secretly, as disappointed as Marianne's.

Deeply as Jane Austen felt for Marianne, victim of a cruel trifler, and sympathetically as she described the poor girls affliction, she could not resist a comic touch. Elinor, appalled by her sister's broken-hearted weeping, could only burst into tears herself, crying so compulsively that even Marianne was roused from her self-absorption to apologise for the unhappiness she had caused her sister. Although Elinor thought it surprising that Willoughby had not declared himself to be Marianne's suitor, she had thought it the prudence of a rather self-indulgent young man, unwilling to commit herself to matrimony, until he had the inheritance he expected firmly assured. This display of perfidy was beyond her imagination. She had come to London to protect her sister from imprudence. She had now to face a far more devastating situation.

The first visitor to call on Mrs Jennings had been Colonel Brandon. He had previously confided to Elinor that Marianne reminded him of a girl, long dead, who had obviously been his first love. He had also inquired if Marianne had any deep aversions to second attachments. Elinor was obliged to admit that Marianne had a prejudice against them, though this was surely unreasonable, as she was herself the child of a second marriage. By these confidences, Colonel Brandon had established a friendship with Elinor which made it not impertinent to inquire if Marianne was actually engaged to Willoughby. At that moment, Elinor could only reply that she did not doubt the strength of their devotion to each other, but had no exact knowledge of the terms on which they stood. Colonel Brandon had said no more, except to wish Marianne every happiness, and to hope that Willoughby 'might endeavour to deserve her'. When Willoughby's treachery became widely known, Elinor was not surprised that Colonel Brandon should call again, but she was intensely shocked by the story he came to tell.

The lady of whom Marianne had so strongly reminded the Colonel was his cousin, Eliza Williams. They had loved each other, and were on the point of eloping to Scotland and an immediate marriage, when they were betrayed and separated. The young man was sent on foreign service, while Eliza was bullied into marrying his elder brother, her fortune being of importance to the family. Serving abroad, the Colonel could be of no help to his sister-in-law. He could only grieve to hear that she had been divorced by her unkind rake of her husband, and had sunk out of sight. When Colonel Brandon eventually returned, he found that his brother knew nothing of his former wife, except that she had transferred the pittance the law allowed a guilty party to another. This was an indication that she had needed immediate relief. Finally, the Colonel was rewarded for seeking out a former servant, detained in a sponging house, by finding his poor sister-in-law, the love of his youth, also detained in the same house for debt.

It would seem that Eliza Williams had 'come upon the town', but had not made a success of it. Only in her early twenties, she was far advanced in a consumption, to which she soon succumbed. She was nursed with devotion by Colonel Brandon, bequeathing to him her little daughter, Eliza, the child of the affair which had led to her divorce. The story, so far, filled Elinor with pity, but her feelings were mild compared to the shock of the Colonel's next revelation.

Although well aware that Mrs Jennings and the rest of the world regarded his ward, Eliza, as his daughter, he attended carefully to her upbringing. He was all the more appalled when, at the age of sixteen, Eliza disappeared, during a visit to a friend at Bath. For eight months Colonel Brandon could only imagine a fate as disastrous as her mother's. Then, at the breakfast table at Barton Park, he received a letter from Eliza, deserted and in advanced pregnancy. At this point in the story, Elinor guessed the dénouement. Willoughby had seduced Eliza, and left her friendless, while he was paying court to Marianne. No wonder, when Colonel Brandon contemplated Marianne's likeness to Eliza's mother, he should tremble at the thought of what her future might be.

Horrified as she was at this additional nail in Willoughby's moral coffin, Elinor had the curiosity to inquire if Colonel Brandon had seen Willoughby since his desertion of Eliza had been discovered. There had been, she was told, one meeting that honour required from the guardian of the betrayed girl, but as neither was wounded, the duel had passed unnoticed. Elinor 'sighed over the fancied necessity of this, but to a man and a soldier, she presumed not to censure it'. Jane Austen did not reveal whether the duel was fought with pistols or other weapons, nor did she mention the 'friends', as seconds were called, without whom the duel would have been very irregular. Had Willoughby actually achieved the seduction of Marianne, it could be speculated that the Colonel might have felt honour required him to challenge Willoughby yet again.

When Elinor had conveyed this tale of pity and terror to Marianne, it did not do so much to raise her spirits in thankfulness at her escape from an ungrateful traitor as Elinor had hoped. It did, however, soften Marianne's feelings towards Colonel Brandon. To have been on the point of an elopement must certainly have appealed to Marianne's respect for romance. Even the duel, fought though it was against her faithless lover, can hardly have failed to add *élan* to the Colonel's image in Marianne's mind. This change of attitude was the first sign that she could think of anything outside her own misery.

Shortly after the Colonel's disclosures, other members of the cast made their way to London from their separate addresses. The Misses Steele arrived at their uncle's house in Bartlett's Buildings, Holborn. This unfashionable address mattered the less, as they proposed to spend their time in Conduit Street with the Middletons, and in Berkeley Street with Mrs Jennings. Willoughby incidentally lodged in Bond Street. The West End was a small world, and it was later revealed that he had spent much time evading a chance meeting with the Misses Dashwood.

Besides the characters met in earlier chapters and now converged on London, two new members of the cast appeared. Elinor had induced Marianne to come out shopping, to a jeweller's in Sackville Street, identified by Doctor Chapman as Gray and Constable, Jewellers, of 41 Sackville Street, Piccadilly. In her capacity as the business head of the family, Elinor wished to negotiate the exchange of 'a few old-fashioned jewels of her mother's'. The shop was crowded, and while the sisters waited for attention, one of Jane Austen's most sharply drawn comic characters made his appearance.

A young man, described in face and person as being 'of strong natural sterling insignificance', stared at the Misses Dashwood so insolently that Elinor was glad that Marianne's abstraction was too great for her to notice the impertinence. Elinor was next surprised to find her half-brother, John Dashwood, at her elbow. His combined pomposity and parsimony made him rejoice that his sisters had found a rich patroness in Mrs Jennings. Having met Colonel Brandon, he immediately allocated the Colonel as a suitor for Elinor, and would not listen to her denials. He even had the generosity to wish that the Colonel's estate of two thousand a year was double in size. He took the opportunity of a walk to call on the Middletons to explain to Eleanor that a match was being planned for Edward Ferrars with the Honourable

Miss Norton, an heiress with thirty thousand pounds. This scheme was being cooked up by Edward's mother, Mrs Ferrars.

The fusion of Mrs John Dashwood and Lady Middleton was effected by the cold-hearted selfishness which each recognised in the other. Little as the Dashwoods were in the habit of giving anything, they decided that it would be good policy to offer the Middletons a dinner. The servile attentions of the Misses Steele to Lady Middleton's children had won them an invitation to stay in Conduit Street, and thus they became added to the Dashwoods' dinner party.

At the prospect of meeting Mrs Ferrars, Lucy Steele, who never missed an opportunity to torture Elinor, confessed to feelings of the utmost apprehension. She could hardly stand, she said, 'Good gracious! – In a moment I shall see the person that all my happiness depends on – that is to be my mother!' Elinor, keeping a grip on her composure, refrained from suggesting to Lucy that her apprehensions might well be groundless. If Mrs Ferrars' plans came to fruition, what Lucy would be meeting was the prospective mother of the Honourable Miss Norton.

Determined to keep aloof from the Misses Dashwood, Mrs Ferrars unconsciously dug a trap for herself by being affable to Lucy Steele. The end of a distinctly uncomfortable evening was marked by John Dashwood's ineptitude. Zealous in promoting Elinor's suitability as a wife to Colonel Brandon, he pointed out how much Marianne had gone off in looks. Colonel Brandon might not now believe it, he said, but Marianne, not so long ago, had been remarkably handsome. John Dashwood did not know what a serious risk he ran of being called out to fight a duel with Marianne's admirer.

The young man, whose impertinent stare had annoyed Elinor in the jeweller's shop, turned out to be Mr Robert Ferrars, younger brother of Edward, but with none of Edward's diffidence. When introduced to Elinor, at a musical soirée, he expressed envy at her good fortune in living in a cottage, though his idea of a cottage approximated to a stately home. Robert Ferrars then went on to bewail the social inadequacy of his elder brother. He had assured his mother that this was due to her ill-advised step in sending Edward to be educated by Mr Pratt. Westminster School had, he told Elinor, turned Robert himself into a polished man of the world. Elinor, for her part, could not reflect with any satisfaction on the results of Edward's sojourn with Mr Pratt. She could only feel that her love and esteem for Edward must be indeed powerful if it did not fail before the unattractive qualities she met with in his mother, sister, and brother. Their combined worthlessness could be compared to that of the nephews and nieces of the Reverend Thomas Leigh, of whom Jane Austen so deeply disapproved.

When John Dashwood humbly suggested to his wife that Elinor and Marianne should be asked to stay, Fanny showed her usual dexterity in avoiding unwelcome guests. She felt obliged to invite the Misses Steele for a stay in Harley Street, but although she averted the threat of being agreeable to her sisters-in-law, she, unawares, laid a mine that was shortly to explode in the face of the Ferrars family.

Lucy's progress, as an adventuress determined to rise in the world, was always in some danger from the vulgarity of Anne, her elder sister. She, alone, was in the secret of Lucy's engagement to Edward, and with more goodwill than discretion supported her sister's efforts to ingratiate herself with Edward's family. Less sharp-witted than her sister, she assumed that Mrs John Dashwood's condescension in presenting both the Misses Steele with a needle book 'made by some emigrant' meant that Lucy would now be acceptable as a daughter to Mrs Ferrars and a sister to Fanny. As Mrs Jennings described the scene in her inimitable style, 'Nancy, who . . . is a well-meaning creature, but no conjurer, popt it all out.'

Mrs John Dashwood, interrupted in her contemplation of the means by which Edward could be induced to propose to the Honourable Miss Norton, immediately went into hysterics on hearing the news of his engagement to Lucy. The Steele sisters were promptly dismissed to the social limbo of Bartlett's Buildings. Mr Donovan, the apothecary, urgently summoned by John Dashwood, could assure the anxious husband that Fanny was in no actual danger, but Mr Donovan was bidden to stand by. Mrs Ferrars had been sent for as soon as the Steeles, snakes in the grass as they proved to have been, had left the house. Further hysterics were to be expected when the news had been broken to Mrs Ferrars.

Mrs Jennings, ever more attractive a character as the novel developed, was outraged at the behaviour of the Ferrars family. She was indignant as a cousin of Lucy Steele, and she was strongly of the opinion that much too much fuss was being made about rank. She had never allowed her spirits to be affected by the artificial refinement of her daughter, Lady Middleton, or the sneers of her son-in-law, Mr Palmer, but she boiled over when John Dashwood arrived to explain the horrors of the situation to his sisters. John Dashwood's expectation that his sisters would share the feelings of his wife and himself at Edward's deplorable behaviour turned his call into a comic occasion.

Mrs Ferrars, her son-law-explained, had summoned Edward, and appealed to every instinct of self-interest. An estate of £1000 a year, clear of land tax, would be settled on him if he agreed to marry Miss Norton, whose own views seem not to have been considered. When 'matters grew desperate', the settlement was raised to £1200, but Edward stood steadfastly by his engagement. Finally, his mother had announced that his disinheritance would be complete. His own property of £2000 would be his only subsistence, and if he attempted to better his condition his mother would thwart him by every means in her power.

'Here Marianne, in an ecstacy of indignation, clapped her hands together and cried, "Gracious God! can this be possible!" ' Gratified at what he thought Marianne's feelings to be, John Dashwood almost congratulated her on taking such a sound view of Edward's lack of filial submission, and disregard of his own worldly prospects. Mr Dashwood imagined that his sisters would be grateful on hearing that Fanny had actually wished she had had them to stay, instead of harbouring the Misses Steele. He added that Mrs Ferrars had even admitted that Elinor would have been a wife for Edward preferable to Lucy.

It was then that Mrs Jennings showed the warmth and integrity of her nature. She declared Edward's behaviour to be that of an honest man, and that her cousin Lucy deserved a good husband. Always anxious to placate persons of means, John Dashwood found himself in a tangle, wishing to assure Mrs Jennings he meant no disrespect to any kin of hers, while maintaining the impossibility of the marriage.

When Mr Dashwood explained that Mrs Ferrars was even now engaged on settling the estate intended for Edward and Miss Norton on Robert, her younger son, Mrs Jennings again exploded. Revenge it might be, but had a son of hers plagued her, she would certainly not have taken steps to make another son independent. John Dashwood then left, assuring his sisters that they need have no undue concern about his wife's state of health, being totally unaware that only a mortal illness on the part of Fanny could have caused his sisters more than a purely formal anxiety.

When Elinor had broken the news to Marianne that Edward was, in his quiet way, as much a deceiver as Willoughby, the younger sister was so impressed by Elinor's silence and fortitude under such a cruel disappointment that she pulled herself together. She even made an effort to be actively polite to Mrs Jennings. Consequently, after John Dashwood had returned to comfort his horrified wife, Elinor, Marianne and Mrs Jennings were able to settle down to comfortable abuse of the entire Ferrars connection, becoming friendlier together than they had ever been before.

Elinor was brought up-to-date as to the progress of Lucy's affairs by meeting the elder Miss Steele on a fine Sunday in Kensington Gardens. There had been panic in Bartlett's Buildings, Holborn, when, after being cast off by his mother, Edward had not appeared for three days. It seemed that he had then offered Lucy the chance of cancelling her engagement to an almost penniless, disinherited young man, with only the bleakest prospects before him. Knowing Lucy's determined and calculating character, Elinor was not surprised to find that Lucy had blocked this avenue of escape, but she expressed intense shock when she found that the elder Miss Steele had gained the information by listening at the door. The latter failed to understand such delicacy. Lucy, she declared, had often done the same to her.

John Dashwood's misapprehension, that Colonel Brandon was courting Elinor, was shared by Mrs Jennings. She had, perhaps, more excuse, having often seen the Colonel talking seriously to Marianne's sister. Mrs Jennings carried this mistaken belief so far that she sat out of earshot when Colonel Brandon came to call. When he left, she was convinced that he had made Elinor an offer, and they talked at cross-purposes, until Elinor realised that Mrs Jennings believed that they were waiting for Edward Ferrars to be ordained, before arranging the ceremony.

Far from proposing himself as a husband to Elinor, the Colonel had been consulting her as to whether he should offer the living of Delaford, his home, to Edward. He was apologetic about the £200 a year which was all the Rectory could command, with only modest hopes of improvement. The offer came from the Colonel's hopelessly romantic heart, wrung by what he imagined to be an echo of his own first love, seeing Edward and Lucy as cruelly persecuted. It was painful, if piquant, to Elinor that she should be made a channel by which Edward would be rescued from immediate want, but lose his last chance of disentangling himself from Lucy. Colonel Brandon had merely thought of making Edward modestly comfortable as a bachelor. Elinor had far too much knowledge of Lucy's tenacity to doubt her insistence in becoming the wife of Edward, however poverty stricken his first living might be.

Having been charged with delivering Colonel Brandon's offer to Edward, Elinor found herself obliged to do it in person. This led her to feel that she should emphasise to Edward how sympathetic he would find his patron to be as a neighbour. Inevitably, Edward assumed that Colonel Brandon's benevolence was due to his hope of making Elinor his wife. In any case, Edward was not looking forward to his marriage with much cheerfulness, but the prospect became even more depressing when he should be living with Lucy in close proximity to a Mrs Brandon, who would have been his real choice as a wife.

When the news first broke of Edward's disinheritance, Mrs Jennings exclaimed at the pauperdom facing Edward and Lucy. They would, of course, marry on the first £50 a year curacy that Edward might be offered, and then have a child every year. Mrs Jennings mind was running on breeding, as she had just presided at her daughter's confinement. The news that Edward had been presented with the living of Delaford only strengthened her conviction that the marriage would take place immediately after Edward's ordination.

The Ferrars family were deeply shocked at their son and brother being rescued from starvation. John Dashwood put forward the hope that, in reality, Colonel Brandon had sold the living, and that Edward had only been put in to hold it until the minor, for whom it was bought, should be of age. Elinor must have taken some pleasure, in an affair that gave her little, by being able to squash her stepbrother's obliging idea. Bred and brought up among the Cloth, Jane Austen made good use, in her plots, of the disposal of livings.

Mrs Jennings' daughter, Charlotte Palmer, being safely delivered of a son, wished for her mother to accompany her back to Cleveland, the Palmer's home near Bristol. With her usual large-heartedness, Mrs Jennings insisted that the Misses Dashwood should travel with her into Somerset, from whence a long day's journey would take them home to Barton. Willoughby's estate, Combe Magna, also lay in Somerset, but Elinor was able to overcome Marianne's initial shrinking from making even a visit to a county where she had hoped to arrive as a bride. John Dashwood, typically, congratulated the girls on getting a free passage home.

It was at Cleveland that Marianne's sensibility led her to commit an act of folly that was to be nearly fatal. The gardens of Cleveland were well timbered, with a row of Lombardy poplars screening the domestic offices. Marianne rambled among the trees to the boundaries of the grounds, taking melancholy pleasure in a Grecian temple, and a spot from which she could see distant hills. From their summits, she fancied, Combe Magna, home of the faithless Willoughby, might be visible to the eyes of disappointed love.

Not only did Marianne indulge in sorrowful ramblings, but she brought on a chill by neglecting to change her wet shoes and stockings. The chill developed into what appeared to have been a sharp attack of pneumonia. Mrs Palmer removed her child from the risk of infection, and the morose Mr Palmer followed his wife. At home Elinor had found him less consistently surly, though she disapproved of the way he wasted his time at billiards. This game made an appearance in two later books, but Jane Austen does not seem to have had the sort of objection to billiards that Charlotte M. Yonge gave to Guy Morville's grandfather in *The Heir of Redclyffe*. The reformed roué made his grandson promise to refrain from even looking on at a domestic game of billiards.

Although Elinor compared Mr Palmer's finicking behaviour over his meals unfavourably with Edward's simplicity and diffidence, she must have been impressed by his lack of resentment, in being forced from the home to which he had so recently returned. Mrs Jennings showed even more sterling worth than she had previously done. She refused to panic over Marianne's condition, though her prognostications were gloomy. Colonel Brandon, perhaps retired as no military duties claimed him, also seemed to expect that he might see yet another fair flower cut down.

In ever more feverish delusions, Marianne worried that her mother, whom she seemed to expect, might arrive too late. Elinor, in her terror, consulted Colonel Brandon, who had already worked out a plan in his own mind. He volunteered to fetch Mrs Dashwood from Barton, and started as soon as his horses could be brought round. It was then midnight, and the Colonel calculated that he should be able to return, with Mrs Dashwood, by ten o'clock the following night.

Elinor, who had accepted the optimistic assurance of the apothecary now found herself doubting that his latest medicines could save her sister from the extreme danger she appeared to be in. Jane Austen did not describe the composition of the draughts made up for various patients in her novels, but it would be of interest to know exactly what temperature-reducing medicine was administered to Marianne. Happily, the apothecary knew his business. The crisis passed and there was no relapse. Elinor could only sit in thankfulness, remembering the hour at which Colonel Brandon hoped to arrive with her mother.

Accustomed to moving from points as distant as Bath from Kent, there was little Jane Austen did not know about the procuring of post-horses, and the relative capacities of gentlemen's carriages. When she described the details of a journey, she did so with complete authority, and never more clearly than in the most dramatic scene of *Sense and Sensibility*. It seemed to Elinor that her fancy had brought her to believe that she heard a carriage at the door a good two hours before Colonel Brandon had calculated that he might return. When she unbarred a shutter, however, Elinor saw that a coach with four horses was standing outside the door, and she supposed the extra pair of horses would have accounted for the unexpected speed. As a bearer of good news, Elinor rushed into the drawing room, to find its only occupant to be Willoughby.

Although she had laughed at Marianne for the intensity of her preoccupation with Willoughby, in the early days of their acquaintance, Elinor had not, herself, been insensible to his attractive nature. But she was now appalled by his sudden appearance. Etiquette, in any case, would have frowned on a young unmarried lady receiving a gentleman in a house where the host was absent, but Elinor had the additional anxiety of expecting Colonel Brandon. The Colonel's account of his last meeting with Willoughby, 'he to defend, I to punish his conduct', might have led Elinor to fear the consequent effect on Colonel Brandon of meeting Willoughby, now a married man, still, apparently, in pursuit of the girl he had cast off. The Misses Dashwood had already caused great disruption in the Palmers' establishment.

To have Colonel Brandon issuing a repeat of his previous challenge to Willoughby, in Mrs Palmer's drawing-room, would have given Mr Palmer, for once, a reasonable cause of complaint.

The shock of seeing someone in whom she and her family had been so grossly deceived, outrage at Willoughby's behaviour to Marianne and to Eliza Williams, mother of his child, fear of a confrontation with her own mother and Colonel Brandon, startled Elinor out of her usual polite composure. When Willoughby declared that his business was solely with Miss Dashwood, she agreed to sit down, but in the curtest manner bade him be quick in saying what he had come to say.

Elinor had already listened to Colonel Brandon's account of his unhappy love affair, which had led, indirectly, to the birth of the younger Eliza Williams. It was now Willoughby's turn to tell his story. In later novels, Jane Austen found that it was better technique to make revelations by letter, rather than by the strain of a vis-à-vis explanation. She never again set up a scene such as that which took place between Elinor and Willoughby.

Even after he had been told that Marianne was out of danger, Elinor found Willoughby's state to be so peculiar, that she spoke almost soothingly to him, thinking it wise to try to calm a man who appeared to be drunk. Willoughby realised what she suspected, and assured her that he had only paused at Marlborough for 'a nuncheon', a pint of porter with his cold beef. He had travelled from London without any other halt. He then settled down to tell Elinor his story, with, he said, the hope that he might earn some forgiveness from Marianne.

The interview was punctuated by the need for

Elinor to remind Willoughby that he was now a married man. At one moment he even went so far as to hint that, should he ever become free, he might still dream of marrying Marianne, and presumably support her on his first wife's money. Elinor would have none of this improper speculation. Willoughby could only express his aversion to the idea that Marianne might yet be lost to him completely by marrying Colonel Brandon. On the subject of his seduction and abandonment of Eliza Williams, Elinor let him off, it might seem unduly lightly, accepting that the unfortunate girl could have used her limited wits to get in touch with him, and not disallowing Willoughby's contention that, if he was a libertine, Eliza must necessarily be a saint. By this amount of sympathy for his predicament, Elinor managed to dispatch Willoughby before Colonel Brandon returned with Mrs Dashwood.

Rejoicing at the prospect of Marianne's recovery, Mrs Dashwood had news of her own for Elinor. During their long journey together, Colonel Brandon had declared his love for Marianne, and Mrs Dashwood had assured him that such a marriage would fulfil her dearest wish. Mrs Dashwood went so far as to say that there had always been something about Willoughby's eyes which she had not liked. Elinor could remember no such distaste, but she knew, only too well, her mother's resemblance to Marianne in the strength of her feelings to question the truth of past suspicions of Willoughby.

Never one for doing things by halves, Marianne made new resolutions on her return to Barton Cottage. As her health improved, she planned a course of study, six hours a day being her proposed standard. She was even able to listen to Elinor's account of her interview with Willoughby, without falling into melancholy or hysterics. Bad news came. The manservant wrecked the family dinner by reporting that he had seen Miss Lucy Steele in Exeter, now married to Mr Edward Ferrars. Marianne, a loyal sister, did then collapse into hysterics from outrage on Elinor's behalf, but the hysterics were less uncontrollable than in the past.

Although she had thought herself prepared for Edward's marriage, Elinor found the pain to be acute. She was unable to decide if she would prefer to hear that Edward was happy or miserable, the idea of either being a stab to her heart. Some days passed with no cheerful prospect, except that Colonel Brandon might arrive. He could explain how the marriage had come to take place before Edward's ordination, which would enable him to offer Lucy a home at Delaford. It was not, however, Colonel Brandon who rode up to the gate of Barton Cottage. It was Edward.

After talk of the weather, Elinor broke an awkward pause by inquiring if 'Mrs Ferrars' was at Longstaple (the home of Lucy Steele's uncle). Edward took the inquiry to be for his mother, so Elinor was obliged to come out into the open, and inquire for Mrs Edward Ferrars. Then occurred one of the most satisfactory dénouements in the novels of Jane Austen. With intense embarrassment, Edward informed the astonished company that his brother Robert had recently married Miss Lucy Steele. Edward's discomfort was so acute that he ruined a pair of scissors by cutting its sheath to pieces.

On getting the letter from Lucy that announced her marriage to Robert, adding that she was well aware that Edward had ceased to love her, Edward himself forsook the habit of apathetic melancholy. Lack of incentive to be happy had hung like a fog over his behaviour, but he now immediately set off for Barton. He arrived there free from one unauthorised betrothal, and, by proposing to Elinor, immediately contracted another. He had believed that Lucy's insistence on continuing their engagement was evidence of her devotion to himself. Elinor, by now his promised wife, was able to enlighten Edward as to Lucy's wiles, and her determination not to let a sprat escape while she trawled for a mackerel. With an acute assessment of psychological possibilities of the situation, Lucy had captured Robert by a mixture of humility and craftiness.

Robert Ferrars, on hearing of Edward's engagement, had expressed great contempt for Lucy, as an awkward country girl, almost without beauty. Lucy was not, however, a girl to be daunted by a gentleman's initial disdain. She had flattered Robert into paying her a number of visits, with the continuing promise that his eloquence might persuade her to break her engagement. Naturally vain, Robert came to believe that he had supplanted Edward in Lucy's affections. On her side, Lucy saw an opportunity to marry the man who had profited by his brother's disinheritance. Having always despised Edward, Robert enjoyed scoring off him. He was also pleased in asserting the independence given him by his mother's settlement, and in marrying without her knowledge.

From the moment that Lucy had first given Elinor her confidence, the latter had been only too conscious of being an object of jealousy, whom Lucy delighted to torture. The last fling in this most unpleasant game had been thrown by Lucy at Exeter, when she had

announced her marriage to the Dashwoods' manservant. Robert, lurking in the corner of the carriage,
would, Lucy knew, pass for Edward to a man who
knew only the elder Mr Ferrars. Lucy had the vicious
satisfaction of delaying, for a few more days, the
joyous relief that Elinor would feel when she learnt
that Edward was free.

To do Edward justice, as soon as he received
Lucy's impertinent letter, announcing that, in the
language of the period, they were now brother and
sister, he did at once set off to claim Elinor, but it
would be hard not to feel that she was almost too
eager to be placated. For all Jane Austen's emphasis
on Edward's qualities of gentleness and good feeling,
he had never appeared to be anything except a poor
fish, and a wet one at that. Elinor, accustomed to
picking up the pieces in the wake of an overly romantic sister, and to restraining the domestic schemes of
an unduly optimistic mother, may have felt that a
diffident husband would be restful by comparison.

Mrs Jennings' outrage at Lucy's behaviour was
such as might be expected from someone of such a
generous nature, who had befriended two indigent
cousins, and had given her approval of the wedding
of Edward and Lucy. The elder Miss Steele was now
the one who needed help, Lucy having borrowed all
Nancy's money to cut a dash at her wedding to
Robert. Newly married couples were not, at that
date, required to spend a honeymoon totally tête-à-
tête (there is an example in *Mansfield Park*), and Mrs
Jennings thought that Lucy's crossness, in refusing
to take her sister with her in the chaise, an aggrava-
tion of her other offences.

The reconciliation between Edward and his mother
took place without any of the humiliating pleas for

forgiveness suggested by John Dashwood as appropriate, Although this would restore one of her sons to her, Mrs Ferrars, from a predominant fear of appearing too agreeable, took a little while to accept Edward back into the family. She even fought a rearguard action over Edward's marriage to Elinor, for which she had been prepared to compound when he threatened to marry Lucy. The Honourable Miss Norton was put forward for the last time as a better proposition, but it was eventually agreed that £10,000, the sum given with Fanny, should be settled on Edward. This enabled Edward and Elinor to start their married life at a level of comfort which suited their tastes.

Something on a grander scale was, not surprisingly, achieved by Mr and Mrs Robert Ferrars. At his wife's instigation, Robert approached his mother, and, after some slight resistance, found himself once again received as her son. Acceptance of Lucy followed. It would have been disappointing to a reader if Lucy had not succeeded in becoming a daughter to Mrs Ferrars, a daughter to be almost more valued than her own child, Fanny. Lucy's past was buried under her fawning attention to her mother-in-law. Mrs Ferrars might visit Delaford Parsonage, but Elinor was always regarded as an intruder in the family, while Lucy, the penniless adventuress, became a petted favourite. The only jealousy and ill-will to develop was that between Fanny, formerly her mother's favourite, and the upstart Lucy, a just reward for Fanny's original encouragement of the Misses Steele.

Tidying up the loose ends of the story, it could be no surprise to learn that when Marianne finally accepted Colonel Brandon's devotion, she did so whole-heartedly. By the time she was nineteen, Marianne found herself 'placed in a new home, a wife, the mistress of a family and the patroness of a village'. Willoughby had the mortification of knowing that Marianne had become devoted to his old, despised enemy, but Jane Austen had, sometimes, a weak spot for the more rakish of her characters. She allowed the reader to know that Willoughby's wife might not always have been disagreeable. Ever a devotee of horse and hound, Willoughby, had, after all, an unlimited opportunity to spend his wife's money on his own enjoyments.

The one loose end left untied was the fate of the younger Eliza Williams and her child (sex undetermined). Silly and eager to be seduced she may have been, Eliza was indisputably the daughter of Colonel Brandon's first cousin. It can only be speculated that she became part of the 'family' of which Marianne became the mistress. When Jane Austen came to write *Emma*, she included, as an important character, Harriet Smith, known to be the natural daughter of anonymous parents. Any hope that this might form a link with *Sense and Sensibility* must, however, be discounted. Harriet Smith's parentage was eventually proved to be far lower in the social scale than that of Eliza Williams, who, whatever her father may have been, on her mother's side definitely belonged to the landed gentry.

2

Pride and Prejudice

Rather too Light and Bright
and Sparkling

JANE AUSTEN

An American novelist, Helen Howe, began her novel *We Happy Few* by describing a circle of New England intelligentsia, of which the males were all engaged in writing books on Herman Melville. The females, on the other hand, devoted themselves to Jane Austen. One of them went so far as to hand-print quotations from the novels on stuff suitable for scarves, choosing, among others the famous opening sentence of *Pride and Prejudice*: 'It is a truth universally acknowledged that a single man in possession of a good fortune must be in want of a wife.'

In pursuit of this philosophical ideal, Mrs Bennet burst into Mr Bennet's library, where he sat abstracted in thought. She brought the news that a newcomer, Mr Charles Bingley, had rented Netherfield, an imposing house in the neighbourhood of Longbourn, the Bennets' home. Jane Austen referred to *Pride and Prejudice* as her 'darling child', but her portrait of Mrs Bennet was unaffectionate. Margaret Drabble, in 1989, attempted a defence of Mrs Bennet as the real heroine of the novel. Twenty years of marriage to a husband who openly despised her, and the difficulty of marrying her portionless daughters, had not, Margaret Drabble pointed out, dampened Mrs Bennet's eager approach to life. In addition, she kept an excellent table, and made the best of her daughter Lydia's patched-up marriage by giving a bowl of punch to her domestics for their merry-making. Mr Bennet may well have enjoyed the good table, but resented any intrusion into his library.

Mr Bennet's property, in default of a male heir, was entailed on a distant cousin, a gloomy prospect for the future of his five daughters. With the exception of Mary, third in the family, these girls were generally attractive, Jane beautiful, Elizabeth witty, Catherine somewhat over-shadowed by Lydia the noisy youngest. The arrival of a regiment of Militia in Meryton, the local town, had overthrown the far from stable balance of the two youngest Miss Bennets. Their mother's sister was married to an attorney in Meryton, and, though uncle Phillips was described as 'broad-faced, stuffy, breathing port wine', he had the merit of entertaining the Militia officers, as cannon fodder for his nieces.

There was a sharp division between the sisters. Jane and Elizabeth had grown up to be well-bred young women, while Lydia, her mother's favourite, dragged Catherine after her into whatever frivolity was on offer. Mary, who mistakenly thought of herself as a scholar, but had managed to become a pedant, was regarded as a dead weight by both parties. The elder sisters were quite prepared to take trouble to dress well, and Elizabeth was trimming a hat, when Mr Bennet said he hoped it would appeal to Mr Bingley. Under the impression that Mr Bennet would not agree to call on this eligible young man,

Mrs Bennet grumbled that it was absurd to talk of Mr Bingley as the girls would never meet him. It then turned out that Mr Bennet had paid the initial call, unexpected behaviour being one of his defences against the tedium of his wife's society.

Their new neighbour was first to be seen at a ball in Meryton. Wild rumours, that Mr Bingley was bringing a large party, in which ladies would be predominant over gentlemen, were confuted. The new tenant of Netherfield was accompanied only by his two sisters, a brother-in-law, Mr Hurst, and a friend, Mr Fitzwilliam Darcy. He was immediately known to be the owner of a splendid estate in Derbyshire, and an income of £10,000 a year, but these assets, together with a handsome appearance, were not enough to earn the forgiveness of the company for Mr Darcy's disdainful behaviour.

Bingley, immediately enamoured by the beauty of Jane Bennet, tried to persuade his friend that it was his duty to seek a partner, and proposed an introduction to Elizabeth. Darcy dismissed the suggestion in the most wounding terms. He declared Elizabeth's looks to be 'tolerable', but not sufficiently attractive to tempt him, nor did he wish to give 'consequence' to a young lady sitting partnerless. Although he agreed with Bingley that Jane Bennet was superior to the other females present, Darcy made it only too obvious that the social level of Meryton was beneath that on which he would choose to be agreeable.

This was the first move in a lover's chess-game that was to be played between Elizabeth Bennet and Fitzwilliam Darcy, Elizabeth making a good story as having been described as 'tolerable'. She was well able to hold her own when they reached the stage of exchanging conversational pawns. Elizabeth was unaffected when Darcy first began to show signs of interest in her. He was aware that she attracted him, but felt that he was armoured against her charms by the many-faceted vulgarities of Mrs Bennet and her younger daughters.

Two more newcomers to the neighbourhood followed on the arrival of Mr Bingley. Mr Bennet received a letter from Mr William Collins, the cousin on whom the Longbourn estate was entailed. Mr Collins, whose letters were to give an expression to the English language, wrote that he would do himself the honour of paying Longbourn a visit. He had previously felt that it would be unfilial to suggest such a visit, because his late father had seen fit to be on bad terms with Mr Bennet. The style of the letter led Elizabeth to ask her father if Mr Collins could possibly be a sensible man. Mr Bennet replied, 'No, my dear, I think not, I have great hopes of finding him quite the reverse.' Mr Bennet was not to be disappointed.

The second newcomer was George Wickham, a handsome young man, newly commissioned into the Militia quartered at Meryton. He immediately put all the other officers in the shade, and as a foil to the Reverend Mr Collins could not have appeared to more advantage. Even the quick-witted Elizabeth decided that here was an unusually agreeable young man. The first meeting with Wickham was, however, the occasion of an encounter that seemed mysteriously intriguing to the Misses Bennet.

The introduction, by another officer, took place in the street at Meryton, when Bingley and Darcy happened to ride past. They halted, Bingley making inquiries about Jane's health, when Darcy and Wickham caught sight of each other. Both changed colour, and the curtest of salutes passed between them. At the first opportunity, Elizabeth made it her business to find out the reason for this coldness of demeanour.

An evening party of Mrs Bennet's sister, the wife of Phillips the attorney, gave Elizabeth the opportunity to inquire into the obviously strained relations between Mr Darcy, who she regarded without affection, and Mr Wickham to whom she felt a distinct attraction. Mr Collins also attended the party, and compared Mrs Phillips' drawing room to the small summer breakfast parlour at Rosings. The hostess did not, at first, accept this comparison as a compliment, but when she found that Rosings was the stately home of Lady Catherine de Bourgh, patroness, religiously and socially, of Mr Collins, she was able to feel flattered by the parallel.

In Jane Austen's gallery of unreliable young men, George Wickham might be counted as one of the most immoral. Willoughby (*Sense and Sensibility*) behaved despicably, but showed some compunction, even though wallowing in self-pity. As will be seen, Henry Crawford (*Mansfield Park*) although prepared to trifle with the feelings of any girl besotted by his charm, could also value goodness of heart strongly enough to propose marrying the penniless Fanny Price. Captain Tilney (*Northanger Abbey*) was prepared to flirt with a girl engaged to another man, but not so seriously as to make his mark as a villain. William Elliot (*Persuasion*) was scheming and coldheartedly false to former benefactors, but he lacked Wickham's irresponsibility. Mr Elliot was a successful fortune-hunter, while Wickham failed so miserably in this field that he could only elope with a young lady as feckless as himself.

Shortly before Wickham's arrival in the neighbourhood, Jane Bennet had spent a week at Netherfield, laid up with a bad cold. Bingley's sisters, the unmarried Caroline and Louisa, wife of Mr Hurst, had taken the girl, so obviously admired by their brother, under their patronage. Elizabeth came to Netherfield to nurse Jane, and so spent some days under the same roof as Mr Darcy. Much to Caroline Bingley's chagrin, Darcy spoke admiringly of Elizabeth's 'fine eyes'. Miss Bingley had set her sights on Darcy, and took much trouble to make herself out to be a bosom friend of Darcy's sister Georgiana. Miss Bingley had always treated Elizabeth in an off-hand manner. This now changed to active dislike, addressing her as 'Miss Eliza', while 'Lizzie' was the family abbreviation. Acute as she was, Elizabeth failed to realise Darcy's tentative admiration for herself, but she thoroughly enjoyed Bingley's mild ragging of Darcy, when Bingley declared, that 'he knew no more awful object than Darcy, on particular occasions, and in particular places; at his own house especially, and of a Sunday evening when he has nothing to do.'

After this experience, Elizabeth was an ideal listener to Wickham's story of his brutal treatment at the hands of Mr Darcy of Pemberley. Had the tale not been told by a handsome young man, Elizabeth might have found the method of its telling a trifle slimey. As it was, she listened with horrified pity to Wickham's account of his early life as son of the steward to the Pemberley estate, and godson of Mr George Darcy, its then owner. Wickham, according to himself, had hoped to enter the Church, and had the assurance from his godfather that a living would be presented to him. But, when the living fell vacant after the death of Mr Darcy senior, his son saw fit to give it elsewhere.

Much shocked by this behaviour, Elizabeth declared that, though she had found Mr Darcy to be haughty, she would never have believed him to be capable of such callous behaviour. Wickham coped with this opinion by explaining that it was pride which prompted Darcy to be kind to his tenants, and affectionate to his sister. Needing distraction after such a disappointment, Wickham had joined the Militia. Society, he hoped, might cheer spirits depressed by the loss of his career. Gratified by being the first person in Meryton to hear this tale of woe, Elizabeth made the mistake of feeling that Wickham's charm could belong only to a truthful nature. She referred obliquely to the matter in conversation with Darcy, and, in reply, Darcy expressed the hope that Wickham's gift for making friends might extend to keeping them. This warning was brushed aside, as being an attempt to justify a guilty action on the part of Mr Darcy.

Ever hospitable, Charles Bingley decided to give a ball at Netherfield to repay the kind attentions of his new neighbours. On this occasion, it seemed to Elizabeth that her family, with the exception of Jane, managed to cause her as much embarrassment as if they had conspired together to outdo each other. Mrs Bennet talked loudly to her neighbour, Lady Lucas, as to the blessing of having a daughter well settled, expatiating on the prospect of Jane's marriage to Bingley, within the hearing of the obviously disgusted Mr Darcy.

Mr Collins then made the discovery that Mr Fitzwilliam Darcy was the nephew of his patroness, Lady Catherine de Bourgh, and insisted in presenting himself, in spite of Elizabeth's pleas that the first move should be made by the person of most consequence.

Elizabeth had begun to suspect that Mr Collins had matrimonial intentions towards herself, and these suspicions were confirmed by his persecutions, which prevented her from accepting any other partner. She was already disappointed that Wickham was absent, feeling, he said, that it would be insupportable to be at the same ball as Mr Darcy.

Charlotte Lucas, the daughter of Sir William and Lady Lucas, and Elizabeth's best friend, was obliging in listening to Mr Collins' saga of the charms of his parsonage, and the affability and condescension of Lady Catherine de Bourgh. Charlotte Lucas had little beauty, and, though of considerable intelligence, seemed, at the age of twenty-seven, to be destined for perpetual spinsterhood. A final display of ineptitude by the Bennet family came from Mary, who, weak in voice and talent, continued to sing until her father put a stop to the insipid performance.

The next morning any after-the-ball lassitude was dispelled by Mr Collins' proposal of marriage to Elizabeth. In the greatest comic sequence of this particular novel, Mr Collins laid out the prospect he had to offer in what he assumed to be irresistible terms. Among the baits for a future Mrs Collins was the assured patronage of Lady Catherine de Bourgh. Regarding his proposal as some compensation for his eventual inheritance of her father's estate, Mr Collins told Elizabeth that, once married, no reproach would pass his lips as to the smallness of her dowry. He was well aware that this was only £1000 in the 4 percents, and that not available in the lifetime of Mrs Bennet.

At that date, a solemn proposal required an answer in suitably grave terms. Elizabeth expressed herself as deeply conscious of the honour done to her by Mr

Collins, but declared she could only decline his offer. To get this refusal spoken was difficult, only by a firm interruption was Mr Collins' loquacity momentarily stopped. She then had to contend with her suitor's conviction that all elegant young ladies showed their delicacy by one, if not more, rejection of addresses which it was their real intention to accept. Nothing would convince Mr Collins that Elizabeth meant exactly what she said, even the plainest language found him assuring her that he expected his next application to be accepted. Elizabeth left the room, feeling that she might have to call upon her father to reinforce her negative, which 'could not at least be mistaken for the affectation and coquetry of an elegant female'.

As things turned out, Mr Bennet's involvement in the drama was not exactly as Elizabeth thought it might be. Mrs Bennet, on seeing that Elizabeth had left Mr Collins by himself, bustled in to congratulate him on the prospect of their closer relationship. He was pleased to accept her good wishes, but she found, only too soon, that he was taking too hopeful a view of the situation. Realising that her least loved daughter, Lizzie, had refused an unexceptional offer, Mrs Bennet assured Mr Collins that Elizabeth 'a headstrong foolish girl' should be made to accept him. Mr Collins, not unreasonably, began to backpedal, considering such characteristics inimical to a comfortable state of matrimony.

Bursting in on Mr Bennet in his library, Mrs Bennet demanded that he should at once force Elizabeth to accept Mr Collins, who was showing ominous signs of changing his mind. Elizabeth was summoned, and, having been assured by her mother that her mother would never see her daughter again if she refused Mr Collins, she was told by her father that she must henceforth be a stranger to one of her parents. He would certainly not see her again did she accept this grotesque suitor. Mrs Bennet's nerves had had a particularly bad day, and their condition was not improved by Mr Collins' determination to remain at Longbourn until the date he had proposed when inviting himself.

This gave an opportunity for Charlotte Lucas *à se ranger*. She deduced that, as Mr Collins had come to Longbourn with the intention of marrying, he would fall easily to the determined approach of a lady, whose single object was to secure the establishment which a husband would supply. If Jane Austen was prepared to allow Marianne Dashwood (*Sense and Sensibility*) as a beauty of nineteen to marry an excellent, if unexciting husband, she was equally prepared to allow Charlotte Lucas, no beauty and twenty-seven years old, to do the best she could for herself. In the three days left of Mr Collins' visit, Charlotte moved so skilfully, yet so quietly, that Elizabeth thanked her for kindly occupying the attention of a guest in the awkward position of a rejected wooer.

Sir William Lucas, father of Charlotte, had been Mayor of Meryton, and, in that office, had been knighted on presenting a loyal address to the King, presumably before George the Third had retreated into mental disarray. His knighthood had induced Sir William, who had made an adequate fortune in trade, to set up house in the newly named Lucas Lodge, and to concentrate on civility to all the world. As has been seen, Charlotte and Elizabeth were friends of higher intelligence than the company they mostly kept. Consequently, when Charlotte announced that she had agreed to marry Mr Collins, Elizabeth's first exclamation was 'Impossible!'

This feeling of disbelief was no more than Miss Lucas expected, but Jane Austen took the opportunity to put into Charlotte's mouth a disquisition on matrimony which must have come from the author's own observation. Not being romantic, and, it was inferred, lacking the looks to encourage sexual attraction, Charlotte considered there to be no reason why she should not have as much change of happiness with Mr Collins, 'as most people can boast on entering the marriage state'.

To this sternly practical assessment of the situation, Elizabeth could only answer, 'Undoubtedly', and she faced the prospect of the loss of sympathy with someone who could take on Mr Collins in the cold-blooded pursuit of an establishment. Elizabeth was not prepared to make allowances for Charlotte's wish for an escape from a home where she was likely to degenerate into an unpaid nurse and cook. Marriage would give Charlotte her own kingdom, and if the price was to endure Mr Collins as a consort, she was prepared to pay it.

The unreliability of female friends was made even more distressingly clear by an oleaginous letter from Caroline Bingley to Jane Bennet. This not only announced the departure from Netherfield of her brother and the entire party, but included yet another 'keep off the grass' notice. Mr Darcy was anxious to see his sister Georgiana, Miss Bingley wrote, and she confided to her dearest Jane that she and Mrs Hurst had hopes that Miss Darcy, a paragon of grace and accomplishment, might be, in the near future, the bride of their brother Charles. Jane, gentle and unassertive, took this to mean that Caroline, her warmly professed friend, had no idea that Bingley might be attracted to Jane herself. Elizabeth, sharper in every sense, interpreted the move to London as part of Miss Bingley's strategy to capture Mr Darcy on her own behalf.

The defection of Bingley, and Mr Collins' engagement to Miss Lucas, were a double trial for Mrs Bennet's nerves. Additionally, she had to support frequent calls from Lady Lucas, who was able to pay off old scores, by rejoicing that she now had a daughter on the brink of matrimony. Mr Collins was anxious to carry off Charlotte into Kent, and, as Jane Austen pointed out, his courtship was not one that his betrothed could wish prolonged. His letters of thanks for hospitality, which has caused the word 'Collins' to be equated with a 'bread and butter' letter, gave much enjoyment to Mr Bennet, a connoisseur of the absurd.

Mr Bennet also found some satisfaction in the marriage of Charlotte to Mr Collins. He had always considered Charlotte Lucas to be reasonably sensible. Now he found that she was as foolish as his wife, and more foolish than his daughter. Mrs Bennet was further tried by the consciousness that Lady Lucas would be calculating the possible date of Mr Bennet's demise, and her son-in-law's consequent inheritance of Longbourn. Mrs Bennet was not comforted in her picture of herself as a homeless widow by her husband's suggestion that she might predecease him, and so avoid such a painful future.

Before she left for her new home, Charlotte extracted a promise from Elizabeth to visit her in Kent. Sir William Lucas, and Charlotte's younger sister Maria, were to visit her in the spring, and, though far from attracted by the prospect, friendship obliged Elizabeth to promise to join the party. Charlotte's letters from Kent expressed satisfaction with the parsonage, and emphasised that Lady Catherine de Bourgh had bestowed every attention on the young couple.

If Mrs Bennet, and her sister Mrs Phillips, had a lack of refinement distasteful to Darcy and the Bingley sisters, their brother, Mr Gardiner, was of a different calibre. Although he lived in Gracechurch Street, in sight of his warehouses, he and his wife were a cultivated and intelligent couple, Mrs Gardiner being a special friend of Jane and Elizabeth. The Gardiner family arrived for Christmas, and Mrs Bennet at once bewailed to her sister-in-law the failure of Bingley to come up to scratch. Mrs Gardiner suggested taking Jane to London, not in pursuit of the fickle young man, but as a tonic for her spirits. Mrs Gardiner was also pleased to meet George Wickham, as she had lived for a happy period of her life in the neighbourhood of Pemberley, the Derbyshire seat of the Darcy family.

Mrs Gardiner was, however, apprehensive that her niece (or neice, as Jane Austen sometimes spelt it) was becoming too much bewitched by the penniless George Wickham. Although willing to admit that she found Wickham exceptionally agreeable, Elizabeth accepted her aunt's caution with the cheerfulness that was part of her nature. Soon afterwards she was able to demonstrate that her aunt's fears were groundless. Wickham, she wrote, had transferred his attentions to a freckled Miss King, recent inheritrix of £10,000. This was regarded as a modest fortune by Jane Austen, which would display Wickham's willingness to settle for a modest heiress. Elizabeth wrote that she felt less disconsolate over this defection than her younger sisters. She described them as 'not yet open to the mortifying conviction that handsome young men must have something to live on as well as the plain'.

If she was a less than cautious judge of her own affairs, Elizabeth was proved to be only too accurate in her suspicions of the professions of friendship offered by Bingley's sisters. In London, Jane had found herself treated as a superfluous country cousin. She had been given to understand that Bingley knew she was in London, but he made no attempt to see her. His sisters continued to emphasise that his close association with Mr Darcy threw him much into the company of Miss Darcy. This was the situation when Elizabeth passed through London in the company of Charlotte's father and sister. Wickham, on saying goodbye, had shown himself to be amiable and pleasing, as he had on first meeting Elizabeth. She was on her guard, but accepted his warning of the arrogance to be expected from Lady Catherine de Bourgh. He had already passed on the rumour that Miss de Bourgh was booked to marry her cousin Fitzwilliam Darcy, and so unite her estate of Rosings with that of Pemberley.

Mr Collins was modestly expectant that Lady Catherine would not be slow in inviting the visitors from Hertfordshire to Rosings, but he was particularly gratified when Miss de Bourgh delivered an invitation to dinner in person. Accompanied by her former governess, still in attendance as a companion, Miss de Bourgh halted her pony carriage outside the parsonage. This happened frequently, but the young lady rarely condescended to enter the house. Elizabeth thought Miss de Bourgh ailing and cross in appearance, and bad-mannered to keep Charlotte standing in a high wind. Miss de Bourgh would, Elizabeth thought, be a suitable penance, as a wife, for the insufferable Mr Darcy.

The dinner at Rosings was the occasion when Lady Catherine originally set eyes on Miss Elizabeth Bennet, whom she was later to regard with virulent dislike. At first, she was prepared to be patronisingly gracious, regarding Elizabeth as 'a very pretty genteel kind of girl'. She subjected her guest to a cross-examination as to her family, and though she expressed pleasure that Longbourn was entailed on Mr Collins, she mentioned that leaving estates away from the female line had 'not been thought necessary in Sir Lewis de Bourgh's family'. She disapproved, in principle, when she heard that all the younger Bennets had 'come out' before their elders had married. Elizabeth was not particularly attached to the bouncing Lydia, but felt that justice required her to protest at the idea of the younger girls being deprived of the pleasures of society, because their elders had not the opportunity to marry.

Elizabeth's manner of expressing her opinion somewhat astounded Lady Catherine, accustomed to the fawning agreement of Mr Collins. Even greater was her astonishment when Elizabeth parried a direct question as to her actual age. She kept to herself the outrage she felt at this display of arrogance and impertinence. In consequence, Mr Collins felt that she must have been impressed by what, in refusing him, she had additionally turned down. Elizabeth did her best to admire what she had seen at Rosings, but Mr Collins found that he had soon to take the eulogy of Lady Catherine into his own hands.

It would be difficult to feel that Jane Austen, known to laugh as she wrote, did not thoroughly enjoy describing the Collins menage. Having, herself, refused the position of Mrs Collins, Elizabeth had a natural interest to see how Charlotte was dealing with a husband, whose egregious manners were equalled only by his conviction of his own right judgement on all questions. Elizabeth had to admit that Charlotte showed considerable ingenuity in softening the impact of life with Mr Collins. His passionate interest in whoever passed his house, particularly if it should be an emissary from Rosings, caused him to spend much time at his study window. Charlotte had chosen a less attractive room for the family sitting-room, but one without a view of the lane, which meant that Mr Collins did not disturb his wife and her guests. He was active in the garden, and Charlotte, with a dead-pan air, talked of encouraging this useful exercise as beneficial to her husband's health. It had also the unmentioned advantage of keeping him out of the house.

Poultry yards played a considerable part in the lives of Jane Austen's female characters. The perpetually laughing Mrs Palmer (*Sense and Sensibility*) thought it wildly hilarious to return home to find that a fox had wrought havoc among her chickens. Mrs Norris (*Mansfield Park*) was given, 'spunged' as her niece Maria remarked, a clutch of pheasants eggs, from which she hoped to raise a brood of chicks. While her successor at Mansfield Parsonage, Mrs Grant, filled the empty corner of her childless home with choice poultry to tempt Doctor Grant's appetite. The turkey, which played an important part in emancipating Fanny Price, was presumably bred by Mrs Grant herself. In *Pride and Prejudice*, however, Charlotte's poultry yard is regarded by Elizabeth as one of the compensations for being yoked to Mr Collins. Presiding over her feathered flock, Charlotte would, at least, have the company of living creatures unable to cause her social embarrassment.

Although to Lady Catherine, Mr Collins must have represented 'the poor man at the gate', she did not behave with the negligence of Dives. We shall never know what would have been Lazarus' response had he actually been invited to share the sumptuous fare of Dives, but Mr Collins accepted every invitation from Lady Catherine. While Elizabeth was his guest, the party from the parsonage dined at Rosings nine times in six weeks, Mr Collins calling there additionally almost daily. The only break in Lady Catherine's insistence on the constant attendance of her courtiers came when her nephews, Fitzwilliam Darcy, and Colonel Fitzwilliam, younger son of Lady Catherine's brother Lord – , arrived for a visit. Indeed she showed irritation that Mr Darcy was already a familiar sight to Elizabeth and the Lucas sisters.

Charlotte may have had a plain face, but she was more alert to the finesse of attraction between the sexes than her friend Elizabeth. She had warned Elizabeth that Jane's 'complaisance' might well deceive Bingley as to Jane's feelings. It had only taken Charlotte three days to transfer Mr Collins' proposal to herself. With the same gift for gauging the feelings of the opposite sex, Charlotte quickly spotted that Mr Darcy was far from indifferent to Elizabeth, in spite of the latter's disdain.

Lady Catherine's nephews found that a visit to Rosings was hard on their nerves, and they frequently took refuge in the parsonage. Colonel Fitzwilliam, yet another Colonel with free time on his hands, made it obvious that he found Mrs Collins' pretty friend attractive. His liveliness was in contrast to Darcy's reserve, which made even the most platitudinous conversation a burden. Colonel Fitzwilliam had the added advantage of not being the eligible owner of a great estate. In fact, meeting Elizabeth on a ramble through the Rosings park, he made his position as a fortune hunter entirely clear, giving himself a licence for flirtation which Elizabeth appreciated.

It was two other remarks by Colonel Fitzwilliam which both upset Elizabeth and made her curious. Discussing the domination exercised by Darcy over his friends, Colonel Fitzwilliam said that he understood that Darcy had influenced his friend Bingley to withdraw from an undesirable courtship. The low connections and the deplorable behaviour of the young lady's family had convinced Darcy that it would be an act of friendship to remove Bingley from temptation.

Elizabeth swelled with resentment at an act that had made her amiable sister so unhappy, and this blotted out her earlier surprise at Colonel Fitzwilliam's reaction when discussing Miss Darcy. He was the joint guardian of Georgiana Darcy, and seemed discomposed when Elizabeth made a frivolous inquiry if, like other young ladies, she was hard to control. She gave the matter no more thought, and returned to brooding on Darcy's high-handed behaviour, exasperation leading to tears, and too bad a headache to allow her to dine at Rosings.

Sitting alone in contemplation of the wreck of Jane's happiness, she was staggered when the perpetrator of the wreck walked into the parlour. Not only did he walk in, but he no longer sat in his customary silence. He immediately announced to

Elizabeth that he had become unable to control feelings against which he had battled. This was an unpromising beginning to the proposal that followed. Disregarding the inequality of their stations, he told Elizabeth that he most earnestly desired to marry her.

On page 2 of *Pride and Prejudice*, Mr Bennet made it plain that 'his little Lizzie' was his favourite daughter. He ascribed his preference to the fact that she had more quickness of wit than her sisters. It would seem to be the case that Elizabeth had inherited this quickness from her father, but she was also the daughter of an impetuous, free-spoken mother. Some of Mrs Bennet's flow of language came to the surface when her daughter startled Mr Darcy by her rebuff of his offer. He had earlier pretended to be uncertain of her reply, but it was clear to Elizabeth that he had no real doubts. He obviously expected her to be humbly grateful for his condescension in overcoming his disdain for the characters and occupations of her connections.

Distracted as Mrs Bennet might have been had she known that her least favourite daughter was refusing the owner of a great estate, with an income of £10,000 a year, she would at least have been gratified by Elizabeth's forthright setting down of her suitor. She assured Darcy that even had he made his proposal in a more 'gentlemanlike' manner, she would still have refused to entertain the idea of marrying him. This final repulsion came after she had accused Darcy of ruining the happiness of her beloved sister by separating Bingley from Jane, and additionally of reducing George Wickham to penury by ignoring Mr Darcy senior's testamentary instructions.

Darcy and Colonel Fitzwilliam were to leave

Rosings in two days time. Wishing to avoid them both, Elizabeth chose a path outside the park for the walk that was to calm her spirits. Darcy, however, managed to track her down, handing her a letter which was to topple the tower of Elizabeth's prejudice against the owner of Pemberley. As she read the letter conviction grew that she was being told the truth. Even Darcy's account of his intervention between Bingley and Jane, she felt obliged to accept. Charlotte had warned her that Jane's pleasant reserve could easily be mistaken for indifference, and this, it appeared was what had happened.

If Darcy's explanation of his interference in Bingley's affairs had shaken Elizabeth's resentment, Darcy's account of his own dealings with George Wickham was even more upsetting to her preconceived ideas. Mr Darcy, senior, 'an excellent father', but evidently lacking in observation, had been easily charmed by young George Wickham, the son of his steward, and to whom he had stood godfather. Mr Wickham, father of George, had been a respectable man, burdened with an extravagant wife. George received a gentleman's education only because his godfather paid the fees for school and Cambridge. George's future was thought to be assured by the prospect of ordination, and presentation to a living in Mr Darcy senior's gift.

George Wickham's story, repeated to most of Meryton, had been that, when the living for which he was intended fell vacant, Fitzwilliam Darcy had refused to honour his father's bequest. Elizabeth now learnt that Wickham had compounded the living for the sum of £3000, to finance his legal studies. Growing up with Wickham as a contemporary, Darcy had long known that Wickham was unsuitable to be a clergyman, but he found himself unable to disturb his father's affection for the young man by giving direct evidence of vicious courses.

Having spent the money intended to support his studies in the law, Wickham then announced that he wished to be ordained, asserting his right to the living for which he had already compounded. Darcy's persistent refusal had led Wickham to attempt a particularly unpleasant revenge, relying on his experience in charming women. Georgiana Darcy, at the age of fifteen, had been set up in an establishment of her own, chaperoned by a Mrs Younge. It has to be accepted that Darcy had been hoodwinked as to the character he chose as duenna to his sister. She was, in fact, secretly in alliance with George Wickham, and promoted him in a courtship of Georgiana. This latter had happy memories of Wickham's kind attentions in her childhood. On that he built an edifice of loving devotion, which charmed Georgiana into agreeing to an elopement. Her fortune of £30,000 (Jane Austen's standard of an impressive *dôt*) would be both a far better support than any clerical preferment, and a fine wound to Darcy's pride as a guardian of his sister.

Watering places were rich coverts where fortune-hunters, of either sex, might hope to flush out a fat quarry. It was at Ramsgate that Wickham persuaded Miss Darcy that only an elopement would prove her love to be completely his. The scheme was thwarted when her brother arrived unexpectedly, and she found it impossible not to confide in him. Jane Austen did not give an account of the scene between Darcy and Wickham. She was scrupulous in not, as it were, writing outside her own experience, which, she considered, barred her from giving a dialogue between two men. Enraged as both men must have been, neither thought a duel to be necessary, no seduction having taken place, as it had in *Sense and Sensibility*.

With this startlingly scandalous knowledge to digest, Elizabeth had to keep her counsel in her farewell to Charlotte and Mr Collins. Among other compliments, Mr Collins expressed his pleasure that the intimacy with Rosings must have been as gratifying to Elizabeth as it was to himself, calling the patronage of Lady Catherine 'the sort of extraordinary advantage and blessing which few can boast'.

Although blinded by his obsequiousness towards Lady Catherine, Mr Collins had made a more sensible point than he can have intended. For three weeks Hunsford Parsonage had been visited almost daily by Colonel Fitzwilliam and Mr Darcy, refugees from their aunt's overbearing personality. Elizabeth had thus been in daily contact with two intelligent, well-bred men, superior to her acquaintances in the rough and tumble of Meryton society. This contrast became only too obvious to Elizabeth when, having been reunited with Jane, their father's carriage was sent to meet his eldest daughters at one of those post towns which Jane Austen tantalisingly left – .

Kitty and Lydia had come in the carriage for the purpose of shopping, and were prepared to threat their sisters to a cold collation. For this it was necessary to borrow the money from Jane and Lizzie. Lydia had spent all her money on a bonnet, agreed by all to be hideous, but Lydia proposed to trim it anew. Not that it mattered what she wore, Lydia said, because the –shire Militia were leaving Meryton, and going into camp near Brighton. Delighted as Elizabeth was at the news, she was the more discomposed when Lydia announced with pleasure that Miss King had gone to her uncle in Liverpool, taking her fortune of £10,000 with her, and leaving Wickham without even the hope of this maintenance. Lydia said loudly that no one could care for Miss King, 'nasty, freckled little thing'. Within herself, Elizabeth was shocked to hear what had once been near to her own sentiments so coarsely expressed.

Heartbroken at the barbarity of the War Office in posting the –shire Militia to Brighton, Lydia kept up the pressure on her parents to take the family there. Sea-bathing, Lydia insisted, would improve everybody's health. Mrs Bennet thought this a delightful scheme. Mr Bennet, in his quirky way, replied ambiguously, though he was obviously determined against the idea. Lydia's grief, however, turned to joy, when Mrs Forster, the very young wife of the Colonel, invited the youngest Miss Bennet to go with her to Brighton. To Elizabeth this was such an appalling prospect that, well aware of the anger that would be roused if her proceedings became known, she appealed to her father to ban the visit. She painted the blackest picture of what would be Lydia's behaviour freed from the slight restraints of home, but she found her father unsympathetic to her representations.

Mr Bennet refused to interfere. He told Lizzie that if Lydia was doomed to run wild, there was unlikely to be another occasion on which she could do so with so little trouble and expense to her family. With an unpaternal detachment, he declared that if Lydia's behaviour further deteriorated her family would be authorised to have her locked up for the rest of her life. As a last throw, Elizabeth said that the impropriety of Lydia's behaviour had already blighted the prospects of her elder sisters. Mr Bennet would only comment robustly that it would be a poor fellow who could not stomach a little ridiculousness. Life with Mrs Bennet had not only increased his cynicism, but hardened his sensibilities.

To a practised lady-killer such as Wickham, the loss of even a minor heiress was a challenge to regroup his forces, and enjoy whatever entertainment came immediately to hand. Wickham turned once again to Elizabeth, whose mortification at having been gulled by his amiable manner was increased by these most unwanted attentions. At a last dinner-party before the regiment left Meryton, Elizabeth was driven to indicate that her meetings with Mr Darcy at Rosings had given her more understanding of his character. Obviously alarmed by this *volte face* on Elizabeth's part, Wickham rallied enough to assure her that Darcy's behaviour at Rosings would be modified by his extreme awe of his aunt, and his wish to forward his own marriage to Miss de Bourgh. From her position of superior knowledge, Elizabeth could only smile, and let the matter drop. When she parted from Wickham each behaved civilly, but probably each had a profound wish never to meet again.

Life was more rational after the departure of Lydia and the Militia, and in three weeks, or so, Kitty found herself able to enter Meryton without bursting into tears. Elizabeth did, however, have a prospect of pleasure before her. Her Gardiner aunt and uncle proposed to take her with them on a driving tour of the Lake District, and she felt that mountains and lakes would give perspective to all the discomforts and confusions of the last twelve months.

Mr Gardiner might be in striking contrast in manners and education to his sisters, but he was none the less subject to the constraints of his business. Unhappily, these upset the plans to reach the Lakes. It was then decided that as Mrs Gardiner had a strong affection for Derbyshire the party should go no farther north. Elizabeth was far from pleased, but decided that, as Mr Darcy could have no means of knowing she was passing through, she could, with impunity, visit the county in which Pemberley lay.

Elizabeth's fate dictated, however, that the friends who were the object of Mrs Gardiner's visit to Derbyshire lived only five miles from Pemberley. The Gardiners themselves showed an eagerness to visit Pemberley, the mansion and a wooded park which Elizabeth found she was unable to give her reasons to avoid. Her only protection was an assurance that the family was not yet arrived at Pemberley for the summer. This information was given her by the chambermaid at the inn where the Gardiner party were staying.

It should here be mentioned that a myth grew up about a particular Derbyshire inn, which it has been difficult to contradict. To her intense surprise, in 1958, Elizabeth Jenkins found that a room had been designated as the room in which Jane Austen had written an important part of *Pride and Prejudice*. To Elizabeth Jenkins' telegram of inquiry, as to whether there was any foundation for this suggestion, Doctor Chapman replied, 'No evidence she was ever north of the Trent'. Unfortunately, the legend grew, mushroom like, and the room itself acquired Jane Austen's desk and bookcase. Had she travelled with these cumbersome objects it is hardly likely that she would have abandoned them in the middle of a tour. It can only be hoped that the firm statement from the Committee of the Jane Austen Society, published in the Report of 1965, will be treated as authoritative. The committee emphatically declared that there was no foundation for the legend that Jane Austen ever visited Derbyshire.

Until railways revolutionised travel, a party of gentlefolk, in their own carriage, would have no difficulty in being shown over a famous house, if the family were not thereby inconvenienced. Housekeepers regarded the task of guiding through the house as both a duty, and an augmentation of their wages. When Mr and Mrs Gardiner and their niece arrived at Pemberley they had already visited Blenheim and Chatsworth. There have been attempts to suggest that Pemberley was based on Chatsworth, but as Elizabeth Jenkins has pointed out, Pemberley was a handsome gentleman's seat, but clearly not on the scale of such a palace as Chatsworth.

It was the housekeeper at Pemberley, Mrs Reynolds, whose praise of her master gave added warmth to the feelings towards him that had been growing in Elizabeth's heart. As they progressed through the main apartments, Mrs Reynolds expatiated on Mr Darcy's good temper, and kindness to his dependants. Her comments on Wickham, a favourite of her late master, were lukewarm. Mrs Gardiner had not yet been disabused as to Wickham's character by Elizabeth, but had learnt that he was not well thought of in his own neighbourhood, leaving under a cloud of debts, subsequently discharged by Mr Darcy.

As the party were preparing for an inspection of the grounds, Elizabeth was thrown into confusion by the sudden appearance of Mr Darcy himself. Embarrassment overwhelmed them both, but Darcy

was able to make a few civil inquiries, while Elizabeth felt he could not fail to see her as a spy. She
walked away with her uncle and aunt, only, as they
proceeded along a riverside drive, to see Mr Darcy
once more approaching.

It must have seemed long ago to Elizabeth that Mr
Darcy had spoken slightingly of her mother's family.
He now asked for the honour of an introduction to
her companions. Whatever his surprise at finding
such an eminently presentable couple being not only
uncle and aunt to Elizabeth Bennet, but brother and
sister-in-law to Mrs Bennet and Mrs Phillips, Darcy
bore the introduction with more than formal civility.
Mr Gardiner had been assessing the sport to be found
in the Pemberley trout stream, and its owner
promptly invited him to fish at his pleasure during
his stay in the neighbourhood.

Mr Gardiner accepted the invitation with a mental
reservation, having some suspicion of the caprices of
great landowners. On the contrary, the next advance
came from Mr Darcy himself, who immediately
brought his sister to call at the inn where uncle,
aunt and niece were staying. Georgiana Darcy was
obviously only too anxious to be pleased with Elizabeth having heard much in that lady's praise from
her brother. Bingley, slightly sheepish, next appeared
to pay his respects. Finally, Mr Darcy called on his
sister to invite the party to dine at Pemberley. Mrs
Gardiner, in whose mind a wild surmise concerning
her niece and the owner of Pemberley had blos-
somed, was happy to accept the invitation.

In dealing with etiquette, Jane Austen treated the
question as part of the fabric of society. Newcomers
in a neighbourhood would be called upon, and only
after the call had been returned could they then be

invited to dinner. The rules governing introductions were graded by the importance, in a worldly sense, of the persons concerned. Elizabeth had struggled in vain to convince Mr Collins that it was not for him to introduce himself to Mr Darcy, the greater in consequence. Ladies acknowledged introductions with a curtsey. When taking a final farewell of Mrs Collins' guests, Miss de Bourgh exerted herself to bestow a handshake, an abnormal effort on the part of this apathetic character. With these rules in mind, Mrs Gardiner and Elizabeth agreed that they should return Miss Darcy's call, even though they were to go to dinner on the following day. Anxious though she was to see more of Miss Darcy, Elizabeth knew that Bingley's sisters were at Pemberley, and only too likely to see her as a dangerous invader.

The greeting from the Bingley sisters was as frigid as Elizabeth had expected, merely a curtsey dropped by each. The conversation struggled on by the help of Miss Darcy's duenna, who had replaced Wickham's confederate. A cold inquiry for Elizabeth's family was answered as briefly as it was chillily made. It was only when a collation, 'beautiful pyramids of grapes, nectarines and peaches', had drawn the company together that Mr Darcy joined the party.

His obvious wish that his sister should become friends with Elizabeth caused Miss Bingley to lose her self-control. Mistakenly, she made a sneering reference to the loss the departure of the —shire Militia would be to the Bennet family. Although she dared not mention Wickham's name, she unwittingly caused acute embarrassment to Miss Darcy by reminding the unfortunate girl of her attempted elopement. Darcy himself went red at this inopportune reference to the regiment in which Wickham was serving.

When the visitors had left, Miss Bingley continued her jealous attempt to denigrate Elizabeth. Reminding Darcy of how cheaply he had held her looks on first seeing her at Meryton, she went on to analyse Elizabeth's face, feature by feature, allowing only her teeth to be 'tolerable'. Although 'tolerable' had been the adjective Darcy himself had applied to Elizabeth when he first set eyes on her, like most people he did not relish being reminded of a discarded opinion. He struck back at his tormentor, telling her that he had long since changed his views '. . . it is many months since I have considered her as one of the handsomest women of my acquaintance'. Miss Bingley was then left to digest a bitter pill.

Just as Elizabeth had reason to feel that she and Darcy might soon come to an understanding, her prospect of happiness was shattered by two letters from Jane, written consecutively, but delivered together. The first contained the alarming news that Colonel Forster had sent an express letter (telegrams not yet invented) to break the news that Lydia had eloped to Scotland. Once over the Border, marriage by declaration would be immediately legal, but the shock of Lydia's elopement was doubled by her choice of a partner being none other than George Wickham.

Reeling from this blow, Elizabeth opened the second letter, to find that a reckless flight to Scotland would be a lesser evil. Colonel Forster had made inquiries, and traced the couple only as far as Clapham, where they had, as it were, taken the equivalent of a taxi into London. Jane, the responsible member of her family, begged Elizabeth and the Gardiners to return with all speed to Longbourn, where the distraught family needed all available support.

Struggling to cope with the immediate steps to be taken, Elizabeth was sending a message in pursuit of her uncle and aunt, when Mr Darcy walked into the room. Whether or not he had come to renew his proposal, he realised at once that Elizabeth had had bad news. He proved himself a kindly listener to her self-reproaches at not having revealed all she knew of Wickham's perfidious doings. The burst of tears which at first prevented her from explaining the case to Darcy may have been better evidence than she guessed that she had a feeling heart under her sprightly manner. Though deeply shocked, Darcy could offer little consolation. When he left her, Elizabeth felt that they might never meet again on the terms which had made the last few days so unexpectedly happy.

No one familiar with Mrs Bennet's approach to family troubles would be surprised to hear that Elizabeth returned home to find her sister Jane wrestling with chaos. Mr Bennet had gone to London in the hope, unlikely to be fulfilled, of tracing the runaways. Mrs Bennet was divided between the wish that Mr Bennet would find Wickham and fight a duel with him, and the fear that Wickham might kill her husband. Whereupon, as she proclaimed in horror, the Collins's would immediately take possession of Longbourn. Kitty, who had known something of Lydia's plan, was in disgrace, while Mary had taken refuge in sententiousness.

From Colonel Forster the family learnt that Wickham had bolted owing debts of honour, which he could not pay, a circumstance that shocked even the tolerant Jane. The only light in the black landscape was that, in the letter Lydia had left for Mrs Forster, she declared she was off to Gretna Green. It was, however, only too clear that she had made no demur when taken to London instead. Mr Gardiner took control of the situation, going himself to London, and sending his brother-in-law home. Mr Collins wrote a condoling letter in his inimitable style, stressing how Lydia's behaviour would cast a blight over the matrimonial prospects of her sisters. Mr Collins was particularly glad that Elizabeth's refusal of his proposal had allowed him to escape from the taint of scandal, now attached to the entire family.

When Mr Bennet returned home, he assured his favourite Lizzie that he bore her no grudge for warning him against allowing Lydia to go to Brighton, 'which, considering the event, shows some greatness of mind'. Kitty said, plaintively, that should she be allowed to go to Brighton she would not behave like Lydia. Her father assured her that no such visit would be possible for her. Additionally, he would never again receive an officer in his house, nor allow one to pass through the village. Kitty, dim-witted and believing his threats, began to snivel. Her father relented enough to promise her that, should she be a good girl for ten years, he would then take her to a review.

Two days after Mr Bennet's return, a letter came from Mr Gardiner, which, while it relieved some anxieties, was only satisfactory in giving Lydia's elopement a whitewash of respectability. Mr Gardiner had seen both Wickham and Lydia. The latter expected that they would be married sometime or other, though the former had taken no steps to bring this about. Mr Gardiner had, however, found Wickham prepared to accept a settlement by which Lydia would inherit £1000 on her father's death, and in the meantime be allowed £100 a year by her father. Mr Gardiner wrote that Wickham's circumstances were better than had been thought, and, when his debts were paid, there would be a little money to be added to the settlement on Lydia.

Jane Bennet, always looking for a gleam of sunshine in the worst situation, congratulated her father, but Mr Bennet pointed out that a far larger sum must be involved than Mr Gardiner mentioned. Who but Mr Gardiner could be responsible for this further sum? 'Wickham's a fool if he takes her with less than ten thousand pounds. I should be sorry to think so ill of him at the very beginning of our relationship.' Mr Bennet could only regret that he had never saved from his income. Had he done so the satisfaction of prevailing on 'one of the most worthless young men in Great Britain' to marry his daughter would not have belonged to her uncle.

In 1813, the year in which *Pride and Prejudice* appeared, Jane Austen had cause to apply 'worthless' to a branch of her own family. Her mother's cousin, the Reverend Thomas Leigh of Stoneleigh Abbey, died childless. To quote again from Jane Austen's letter of 3rd July, 1813, 'Mr Thos Leigh . . . died the possessor of one of the finest Estates in England and of more worthless Nephews and Neices than any other private man in the United Kingdom.' George Wickham would obviously have been at home in this circle of cousins.

Mrs Bennet accepted the news that Lydia was to be married with rapture, casting aside her nervous incapacity, and assuring the housekeeper that she and the maids would be given a bowl of punch in celebration. Elizabeth had to take her share of congratulations, while suffering not only from doubts of the couple's future, but the conviction that such a deplorable match had set up an insurmountable barrier between herself and Mr Darcy.

Mrs Bennet hastened to spread the news among her neighbours, disappointing their hopes that, if Lydia did not actually 'come upon the town', she would at least be sequestered in some remote farmhouse. The mother's list of the houses in the neighbourhood suitable for the young Wickhams was halted by Mr Bennet's declaration that there was one house where they were not to enter, Longbourn itself. It needed all the persuasion of Jane and Elizabeth to convince their father that propriety required the couple to be received in the bride's home.

Lydia and Wickham travelled directly to Longbourn after the ceremony. It was to be a short visit, for Wickham had transferred from the Militia to the Regulars, and had been promised an ensigncy in a corps that was stationed in the North. Mrs Bennet was alone in lamenting this move, which distanced her favourite daughter so far from her. The rest of the family could only hope that among strangers, respectability might be maintained. At the moment Lydia was infatuated with her husband, proud of being married before her elder sisters, and unabashed at living with Wickham for weeks before the wedding.

In spite of Lizzie's protests that the less said on the subject the better, Lydia forced her sister to listen to an account of her wedding at St Clement's, without orange or lemon blossom. It was then that Elizabeth learnt to her astonishment that Mr Darcy had been present at the wedding, almost, it seemed, in the capacity of best man to Wickham. Lydia then exclaimed that she had given away a secret, and Jane could only assure her that she would not repeat the fact of Darcy's presence, nor inquire further. Elizabeth could not, however, resist writing to her aunt for an explanation of the extraordinary presence at Wickham's wedding of a man whose dislike of the bridegroom was profound and justified.

Elizabeth learnt from her aunt's reply that, after their parting in Derbyshire, Mr Darcy had gone to London, called at once on Mr Gardiner and explained that he had a clue which might lead to tracing the runaways. Darcy had declared that he regarded himself as responsible for this disaster by having kept his knowledge of Wickham's character to himself. He had been too proud to clear his own reputation of the slur that he had injured Wickham. Through Darcy's knowledge of Wickham's friendship with Mrs Younge, disgraced governess of Miss Darcy, the eloping couple were found. Mrs Gardiner suspected that there had been some bribery by Mr Darcy, before Mrs Younge, now keeping a lodging house, had been willing to supply the address to which she had directed Wickham and Lydia. Her own house which sounds barely respectable, was full, so she had a strong card in her hand when dealing with Mr Darcy, towards whom she must have had a wish to revenge herself.

Elizabeth walked out into the fresh air to read her aunt's long letter. Seated on a bench, she ran through a range of feeling from the contemplation of the nobility of Mr Darcy's behaviour to regret for the harsh words and thoughts she had ever spoken or nursed towards him. She learnt that the money which had rescued Lydia from a disgraceful situation had been provided (with a proviso of secrecy) by Darcy.

There had been some bargaining on Wickham's part, as he still had hopes of capturing an heiress. Mrs Gardiner took the liberty of assuring her niece that she liked Darcy immensely, but felt he might be improved by a lively wife. She hoped this boldness would not lead to her being banned from Pemberley. She had an ambition to go right round the park. 'A low phaeton with a nice little pair of ponies would be the very thing.'

Elizabeth was contemplating the delights of such a prospect, when what she feared to be the main obstacle to its fulfilment appeared before her, Wickham having deliberately followed her with the wish to inquire about Pemberley. There followed a highly comic bout of verbal fencing, neither party letting down their guard. Negligently, Wickham inquired as to whether Mrs Reynolds, the housekeeper at Pemberley – always so fond of him – had happened to mention his name? Elizabeth replied with a smart lunge. Mrs Reynolds, she said, had mentioned that Mr Wickham had gone into the army, 'and she was afraid had-not turned out well. At such a distance, you know, things are strangely misrepresented.'

Although biting his lip with embarrassment at this thrust, Wickham could not restrain himself from probing to discover how much Elizabeth knew of Darcy's involvement in his marriage to Lydia. He mentioned that he had happened to pass Darcy several times in the street, and wondered what brought him to town at such an unfashionable time of year. Elizabeth could false card as well as Wickham, and she blandly suggested that Mr Darcy might have gone to town in the dead season to prepare for his wedding to Miss de Bourgh.

This brush-off did not deter Wickham from inquir-

ing if Elizabeth had met Miss Darcy while in Derbyshire. To which she replied that she had, and had
liked Miss Darcy very much. She must be improved,
Wickham speculated. He had not thought her promising a year or two ago. By this time it must have
been clear to Wickham that Elizabeth knew of his
dealings with Miss Darcy, who, said Elizabeth, must
have not got over the most trying age.

Wickham's final throw was to ask if Elizabeth had
passed by the village of which he had been expected
to be given the living. She suggested that he might
have found it tedious to have to compose sermons,
but Wickham assured her that he would have gladly
fulfilled this duty. Although she had made it clear
that she understood Wickham's behaviour towards
Darcy on this subject, Elizabeth was prepared to offer
her hand as a sisterly gesture. Wickham might be
vanquished, but he was ready to kiss her hand 'with
affectionate gallantry', his lady-killing mechanism
coming into action. Both parties were delighted that
his destination was to be remote Newcastle.

The departure of the young Wickhams was
lamented by no one except Mrs Bennet. Wickham
took a graceful farewell, about which Mr Bennet
remarked that he defied Sir William Lucas himself to
produce a more valuable son-in-law, referring, of
course, to Mr Collins. Mrs Bennet's melancholy was,
however, soon relieved by the news that Mr Bingley
was returning to Netherfield. Jane preserved less than
her usual calm, and Elizabeth found it difficult to
keep her own hopes at bay. Mrs Bennet urged her
husband to call on Bingley at the earliest moment,
but he, with customary perverseness, refused to do
so. He complained that, having called the year before

on the promise that Bingley would marry one of his daughters, nothing had come of it.

It was, in fact, Bingley who made the first call, riding up to the house, and bringing Darcy with him. The embarrassment of the elder Miss Bennets over their mother's over-warm welcome for Bingley, and chilliness towards Darcy, was increased when Lydia's marriage was mentioned. Bingley wished the mother joy, as etiquette required, but Mrs Bennet complained that the notice 'in the Times and the Courier' was awkwardly phrased. She was far from accepting that her brother had made the best of a bad job by inserting an ambiguous notice, 'Lately, George Wickham Esq, to Miss Lydia Bennet'. Mrs Bennet also took a swipe at Darcy, by thanking heaven that Wickham had, at least, *some* friends prepared to help him in his new profession as a regular soldier.

Bingley's visits to Longbourn now became assiduous, and it was not long before Mrs Bennet had the vast satisfaction of learning that he had proposed to Jane. After the murky business of Lydia's wedding, the sun had suddenly come out on the Bennet family. Although he prophesied that Mr and Mrs Charles Bingley would be a soft-hearted couple, imposed on by everybody, even Mr Bennet acknowledged that the match promised to be a happy one.

It was during the first glow of Jane's engagement that a chaise, drawn by four horses, came to the door, and Lady Catherine de Bourgh was ushered into the upstairs parlour. Her manner was at its most arrogant, and though she was obliged to acknowledge the presence of Mrs Bennet and Kitty, it was without civility. After a few constrained moments, she asked Elizabeth to join her on a walk in the grounds, pausing only to approve the other reception rooms, as the prospective property of Mr Collins and Charlotte.

In the interview that followed, Lady Catherine, as a bulldozer, found Elizabeth Bennet uncrushable. Their verbal contest began with Lady Catherine requiring Elizabeth publicly to deny that she was engaged to Mr Darcy. In reply, Elizabeth pointed out that this call from Mr Darcy's aunt would be likely to give plausibility to the rumour. To the announcement that Darcy was engaged to Miss de Bourgh, Elizabeth suggested that it would be surprising for Lady Catherine to think that he had proposed to herself.

'Obstinate, headstrong girl', was about the mildest abuse thrown at Elizabeth by Lady Catherine, when the young lady asserted that, though she was not engaged to Mr Darcy, she would make no promise never to become so. Lady Catherine had insulted Elizabeth by stressing the lack of breeding and consequence in her family, threatening her with ostracism by Mr Darcy's kinsfolk should the marriage take place. Lady Catherine became further exasperated when Elizabeth pointed out that the world would have too much sense to join in such an idiotic policy. Her own situation as the wife of Mr Darcy would, inevitably, be so agreeable that she would have no need to concern herself with the opinions of the de Bourghs. Defeated in the purpose of her visit, Lady Catherine stormed away behind her four horses, declaring that she was too displeased to take even a formal farewell of Elizabeth and her mother.

Warm as Elizabeth's feelings had become towards Mr Darcy, she found that her contempt, freely expressed in the past, now came home to roost, precipitated by a letter from Mr Collins, well up to his usual standard. Congratulations on Jane's engagement, was followed by concern that Lydia and Wickham had been received into her father's house. As a minister of religion, Mr Collins wrote it was his duty to protest at this slurring over of vice, which should be forgiven as a Christian, but the sinners barred from all contact. Illogically, Mr Bennet derided this idea of Christian forgiveness, forgetting that he had had to be persuaded out of the same attitude by Jane and Elizabeth.

Mr Collins' principal reason for writing was, however, to warn the Bennet family that it had been reported that Mr Darcy had offered Elizabeth his hand, and his Pemberley estate. Naturally, Mr Bennet would wish to close at once with this offer, but Mr Collins urged that it would be unwise to hasten into a union not properly sanctioned, Lady Catherine de Bourgh being implacably opposed to such a match. Mr Bennet was surprised, but incredulous. He stuck pins into poor Lizzie by treating as a delusion the idea that Mr Darcy had ever cast his eyes in her direction. Her father went so far as to reproach his daughter for obviously finding the joke less diverting than he did.

Mr Collins continued with the news that Charlotte was expecting what he described as a 'young olive branch'. It has been observed that pregnancy is never, in the scheme of Jane Austen's novels, bestowed on any of her real favourites, none of whom find themselves in an 'interesting situation'. Having married for an establishment, Mrs Collins was not one to shirk her duties. It can be hoped, though never known, that Charlotte's children escaped the inheritance of their mother's plain face, and their father's sententious habit of mind.

Any fear that Mr Darcy might pay attention to his aunt's protests was unfounded. He joined Bingley in a call immediately after Lady Catherine's visit. Elizabeth found herself alone with him on a walk, and, winding up her courage, began a speech of thanks for his kindness to Lydia. Assured that the betrayal had come from an indiscretion of Lydia's, and not from Mrs Gardiner, Darcy declared himself to be unaltered in his affection. When Elizabeth declared that her affection had grown the more she had got to know him, all barriers were down between them. They walked a greater distance than they were aware of, and when they returned to Longbourn it was as the happiest couple in the world.

Elizabeth's next, and final, difficulty was to convince her family that her feelings towards Darcy had changed. Even Jane, who wished for the marriage needed some persuasion and Mr Bennet was much more taken aback. He went so far as to tell Lizzie that he could not bear the thought of her making a worldly match with a man she disliked. He prophesied that the liveliness of her spirits would, if despising her partner in life, lead her into misery and disgrace. When, however, he understood the revolution of her feelings, he fell back into his usual style. Having laughed at Elizabeth for having had to listen to Mr Collins' letter, he summed up the situation. 'I admire all my three sons-in-law highly,' said he, 'Wickham, perhaps, is my favourite; but I think I shall like *your* husband quite as well as Jane's.'

When Jane Austen tidied up the loose ends of *Pride and Prejudice*, she also indulged the reader with hints of future developments. Mrs Bennet remained irredeemably silly, but, the author speculated, Mr Bennet might have found that the acquisition of a sensible wife would have required a painful adjustment of his self-protective philosophy. The distance between Hertfordshire and Derbyshire was seen by Elizabeth as a mercy. Even the good-natured Bingleys soon fled from the embarrassment of Mrs Bennet and Mrs Phillips as near neighbours. Mr Bennet developed the habit of arriving at Pemberley when least expected. Having married a father's favourite child, Darcy had to take the consequences, and learn to appreciate his father's acerbic wit.

Staying with her brother Henry in Sloane Street, in 1813, Jane Austen went with him to the watercolour exhibition. Here she had the pleasure, as she wrote to her sister Cassandra, of finding a small portrait of Mrs Bingley. 'It was excessively like her', and her white dress trimmed with green ornaments, confirmed her creator's belief that green had always been Jane Bennet's favourite colour. A hope of finding Mrs Darcy at two other exhibitions, one of Sir Joshua Reynolds' works, was disappointed. With something of Elizabeth's tendency to laugh at Mr Darcy, Jane Austen contented herself with the supposition that Mr Darcy's feelings of 'Love, Pride and Delicacy' would not allow his wife's portrait to be exposed to public view.

It would be wrong to leave the novel without mentioning that, detached from Lydia's frivolity, Kitty Bennet became 'less insipid'. *The Memoir of Jane Austen* (J. Austen Leigh) revealed that Kitty had the good fortune to marry a clergyman near Pemberley, who presumably would be advanced in the Church by the Darcy influence. Mary, on the other hand, only escaped from being handmaiden to her mother by marrying a clerk in her Uncle Phillips' office. Mary need not be pitied too much, as her accomplishments were probably sufficient to allow her comfortably to look down on her husband, and she could also boast of being the sister of Mrs Fitzwilliam Darcy of Pemberley, Derbyshire.

3

A Stroll Through Mansfield Park

'[Miss Crawford] looked about her with due consideration, and found almost everything in [Tom Bertram's] favour, a park, a real park five miles round, a spacious modern built house, so well placed and well screened as to deserve to be in any collection of gentlemen's seats in the kingdom, and only wanting to be completely new furnished . . .'

When Miss Crawford made this assessment of the seat of Sir Thomas Bertram, with the idea that his eldest son might be a suitable husband, the plot of *Mansfield Park* had been unwinding to cover what was, for Jane Austen, an unusual number of years. In fact, this novel is the nearest that Jane Austen came to writing a family saga, even if she restricted herself to two generations. As the story developed, the 'spacious modern built house' took on the importance of a living character, becoming familiar to the reader as it must have been to the Bertrams themselves.

To have appeared to be modern in the eyes of Miss

Crawford, the house must have been built at the finest moment of English domestic architecture. As she saw it in the early years of the 19th century, it might well have been constructed to celebrate the marriage of Sir Thomas Bertram to Miss Maria Ward. Her fortune was no more than £7000, and, though her beauty was undeniable, her uncle, a lawyer, considered that she was at least £3000 short of a claim to such a match. Presumably, his profession had made him expert in assessing young ladies' dowries. When Lady Bertram arrived at her new home the paint must have been very fresh in the drawing room where she was to spend so much of her life, innocently working at tapestry and fringe.

The nurseries at Mansfield Park were on the top floor and near to the attics. (I. Compton-Burnett has pointed out that this arrangement, mandatory in big houses, compels those with the shortest legs to climb the most stairs.) The nurseries themselves were filled with the decorum that attended the Bertrams's way of life. Two sons, Tom and Edmund, were followed by two daughters, Maria and Julia, after which Lady Bertram appears to have rested on her oars, for which her youngest sister Frances might well have envied her.

The elder sister of Lady Bertram had married the Reverend Mr Norris, to whom Sir Thomas had presented the living of Mansfield. They had an income of about a thousand a year, but Mrs Norris, expected something on the scale of Mansfield Park as an establishment, saw fit to indulge herself in the pleasures of parsimony. Jane Austen excused Mrs Norris from the burden of children, and on becoming acquainted with her character, no one could wish her to have been a mother. Mrs Price, as Miss Frances became, had, on the other hand, an overflowing quiver, whose disposal gave impetus to the novel.

Mr William Price, Lieutenant of Marines, was not a man to appeal to Miss Frances' family as a husband. Having given him a lowly position in society, Jane Austen then incapacitated him by an accident from any chance of rising in his profession. The marriage was announced to Miss Frances' family only after it had taken place. This gave Mrs Norris the opportunity to widen a breach into a chasm.

Her prophecies, that Fanny's rash act would be followed by retribution, turned out to be only too completely fulfilled. At the time, however, Mrs Price took exception to her sister's strictures. Comments on the pride of Sir Thomas reported by Mrs Norris, caused the Price family to be consigned to a limbo at Portsmouth. Ten years passed without contact, although Mrs Norris, chief agent in the estrangement seemed to have had an underground source of information. Sir Thomas was regularly surprised when Mrs Norris angrily announced that Fanny had got another child.

Life at Mansfield Park rolled on sedately. Lady Bertram took no part in the education of her daughters, who were in the care of a governess, while masters instructed them in music and drawing. Their mother sat on a sofa in the drawing room engaged on needlework of 'little use and no beauty', frequently dozing, and only rousing herself to attend to her pug dog, with a care denied to Maria and Julia. Tom and Edmund passed into Eton, and were seventeen and sixteen years of age when the prosperous life at Mansfield was broken into by a reminder that poverty could intrude into a select family circle.

After eleven years of struggle, Mrs Price could not

afford to neglect any possible help for the future of her growing family. Mrs Norris' prophecies had come true to an extent that even her baleful mind might have judged to be excessive. Mrs Price, faced with her ninth lying-in, wrote to implore the help of her sisters and Sir Thomas. Her appeal set in motion a chain of events which was to influence the family at Mansfield beyond anything that could have been forseen.

After writing the letters which accompanied some immediate relief for the Price family, Mrs Norris, whose benevolence operated almost entirely at second hand, put forward an idea of more permanent value. She suggested that the Bertrams and herself might at least relieve Mrs Price of the care of her eldest daughter Fanny, now nine years old. Mrs Norris found no opposition to this scheme from Lady Bertram, but Sir Thomas had some reservations. He looked to a future when provision would have to be made for Fanny, and, more ominously, that his sons might fall in love with their indigent cousin. Mrs Norris talked down these objections, being in love with her own scheme, and determined that all outlay should come from Sir Thomas.

Lady Bertram was not given to surprise, but Sir Thomas found it unexpected that Mrs Norris, who had promoted the adoption plan, should be adamant that it would be impossible to receive little Fanny Price at the Parsonage. The Reverend Mr Norris, his wife explained, was too much of an invalid, suffering from a gouty complaint, to be able to tolerate the disturbance that the child would cause. Having gained her point, Mrs Norris set out for Northampton in the Bertrams' carriage to meet Fanny, the child fated to become the Cinderella of Mansfield Park.

To Fanny the arrival at her new home was overpowering, particularly as the last stage of her long journey was made unnerving by the assurances of her Aunt Norris that no child could be more fortunate. Admonitions to be grateful and happy were underlined by the importance of making a good first impression on her benefactors. Fanny could not then know that her initial experience in this new and alarming circle was, also, in a manner of speaking, a sample of the worst she would have to endure. Whatever troubles were to overtake her in the course of the next ten years, Mrs Norris was certain to be holding the spoon that would stir the witches' cauldron of unkindness.

Edward Austen, brother of Jane, had been adopted by a distant connection, the childless Mr Thomas Knight of Chawton in Hampshire and Godmersham in Kent. Nothing could have been less like the circumstances in which Jane Austen sent her heroine Fanny to live at Mansfield Park, but there might be one hint that her brother's adoption was not entirely out of the author's mind. Mrs Norris went to fetch Fanny with the double idea of being the first to welcome the child, and the beneficent aunt who was to lead her into the Mansfield drawing room. There she would have the gratifying sensation of introducing the newcomer and commending her to the patronage of the assembled Bertrams.

What is probably the best-known among the portraits surviving of the Austen family may have given Edward's sister Jane an idea for the scene. This charming family group was painted in black and gold washes, rather than in the late and degenerate medium of black paper and scissors. The Reverend George Austen urges forward his son Edward towards two ladies, who are seated at a chess board. Mr Knight, with as penetrating a gaze as silhouette would allow, leans over the back of what is, perhaps, Mrs Knight's chair. Edward, himself holds out his hands as one sure of his welcome, as he had every reason to be. Although the artist's grasp of perspective was shaky, the group has much liveliness.

Fanny's first immersion in the Bertram family pool was far less genial. She had come from a cramped house in a narrow street in Portsmouth, and she found the vast drawing room of her new home terrifying. Lady Bertram, seated on the sofa with her pug, did indeed make room for her niece, but the stately manners of Sir Thomas further upset Fanny's composure. The sons of the house appeared to her as young men rather than boys, and the daughters, though not much older than herself, seemed almost equally frightening.

When she had been dispatched, in tears of exhaustion, to the little white attic nominated by Mrs Norris as appropriate for a poor relation, the kind aunt speculated if Fanny might not have inherited some sulkiness of disposition from her mother. Apart from this remark of sisterly spite, Mrs Norris had already sensed the quality of a victim in Fanny. She was in the habit of fawning on her Bertram nieces, who, in any case, were well able to look after themselves. To bully Fanny was to give her love of fault-finding an outlet.

Few novelists have laid out the houses in which their characters live with as much care as Jane Austen, and in Mansfield Park it would not be difficult to draw a plan of the ground floor of Sir Thomas' mansion. The hall was obviously of a good size in proportion to the rest of the house. There was a library, a breakfast-room, and presumably a dining parlour, and a billiard room beyond which lay Sir Thomas' own room, 'his own dear room'. But above all there was the drawing room, background to many of the family dramas. Here Lady Bertram could always be found, a stationary leg of a compass, round which the rest of the household rotated. No one rotated more than Mrs Norris, who behaved like a Queen Stork to her sister's Queen Log.

The little white attic had been suggested for Fanny by Mrs Norris, because the nearby housemaids could care for the little girl. That the room had no fireplace emphasised that Miss Price was not a Miss Bertram and, unpacking her scanty wardrobe, the maids could not refrain from sneering. After a week of loneliness and private tears, Fanny was discovered by her cousin Edmund as she sat crying on the attic stairs. He took the trouble to find out the reason, and so became Fanny's friend, confidant and protector. More immediately, he was useful in helping Fanny to write to her brother William, much the most loved of the family she had left at Portsmouth.

One of Fanny's troubles was the lack of purpose in her new life, after having been a useful eldest sister at home. It was not long, however, before Lady Bertram found her able to take on the duties of a handmaiden, which her own daughters showed little wish to perform. Enabled to live even more placidly than before, Lady Bertram appreciated Fanny's obligingness as a taker of messages, and a needle-woman who could cope with the admittedly simple difficulties of carpet work or fringe.

Maria and Julia were pleased to patronise their

cousin as a creature of a lower grade, sometimes a useful third in their pursuits. Tom Bertram laughed at Fanny, but made her pretty presents. It was, however, Edmund who earned her devotion by listening to her troubles, persuading her to overcome fright at the idea of learning to ride, and choosing books for her further education. His reward was to be a devotion which grew with Fanny's growth, developing, inevitably, into the love which Sir Thomas had apprehended on the part of his sons, but no one, least of all Edmund, suspected the state of Fanny's affections.

After five years at Mansfield Park, Fanny had an unpleasant shock. The Reverend Mr Norris, having failed to conquer his gouty condition, died. His widow was then obliged to quit the parsonage, where a new incumbent was to be instituted. By rights, the living should have been held by some friend of the family until Edmund, destined for the Church, was old enough to take orders. Unfortunately, his elder brother, Tom, had been so recklessly extravagant, and so unlucky a gambler, that the presentation had to be sold to pay Tom's debts. Sir Thomas gave a just rebuke to his elder son, for though Edmund still had the prospects of an inferior living, his presentation to Mansfield must now wait for the death of Doctor Grant, a man only forty-five years old. Tom Bertram, a young gadabout of puppy-like irresponsibility, placated his conscience towards Edmund by reflecting that his father was making an unnecessary fuss, and, anyway, Doctor Grant, from his plethoric appearance was likely to go off, at short notice, in an apoplectic fit.

Financial stress had also come from lack of profit on Sir Thomas' West Indian estates (not their only

appearance in Jane Austen's novels). In these circumstances, Sir Thomas felt that, should Mrs Norris take
Fanny into her home, it would not only relieve him
of Fanny's immediate support, but probably of her
future provision as well. Although it was not yet
generally acknowledged that parsimony was the
main pleasure of Mrs Norris' existence, it was known
that she had always put by savings from her income.
If she took on the care of Fanny, it might seem
reasonable to expect that these savings would eventually form a *dot* for Miss Price.

This solution for the problem of Fanny's future
seemed so satisfactory that Lady Bertram mentioned
it to Fanny as her certain destiny, a shock that caused
great distress to the young girl. Edmund, inured to
the perpetual bustle that attended the doings of his
Aunt Norris, did his best to reassure Fanny. With the
rather priggish insensitiveness which was a counter-
balance to the kindness of his character, Edmund
painted a picture of Mrs Norris encouraging Fanny
from sheltering in the shade of her elder cousins. He
did not seem to have noticed that Mrs Norris took
every opportunity to snub Fanny.

Fanny need not have distressed herself. Mrs Norris
had foreseen the moment when her bluff would be
called over taking her proper share in the adoption
of Fanny. She had deliberately chosen the smallest
house in the village with pretensions of gentility, and
she protected her flank by declaring that she must
always keep a spare room available for a friend. With
some obtuseness, and remembering little entertaining
at the parsonage, Sir Thomas had assumed that this
spare room at the White House would be a suitable
bedroom for Fanny. He was quickly disillusioned.
When Lady Bertram mentioned the matter to Mrs

Norris, the latter exclaimed that no one could be unkind enough to force such a charge on a heartbroken widow. As regards the future, small as her life's savings might be they were intended for Sir Thomas' children, as dear to her as if they had been her own. Hopelessly outmanoeuvred, Sir Thomas could only trust that the prospect of his children being heirs to Mrs Norris might allow him to make some provision for Fanny.

To quote Elizabeth Jenkins, Jane Austen's life was spent in an age when even the most prosaic objects of everyday domesticity, cups, saucers, small village houses, were of a restrained elegance that was to fade into a tangle of styles and fashions. It would not be difficult to imagine the appearance of the White House, which stood across the park from Sir Thomas' mansion. In her husband's lifetime Mrs Norris had had command of an income close on £1000 a year, comfortable means when a schoolmaster might be fortunate to have stipend of eighty pounds on which to keep up a respectable appearance. Even after her husband's death, Mrs Norris, as Sir Thomas told Lady Bertram, would still possess £600 a year, an obstacle in her presentation of herself as an impecunious widow.

As Mrs Norris had chosen the White House so that there would be no room for Fanny, it must be assumed that, in house agent's terms, it would offer two reception rooms and two main bedrooms, one for Mrs Norris and one reserved for the mythical friend. It would not be difficult to visualise the simple white exterior and the graceful proportions of doorway and windows. Nanny, the housekeeper, and at least one underling, would have be stowed away in an attic storey. Still thinking with the mind of a house-agent, the White House could, nowadays, be called a highly desirable residence.

It was from her observation post in the White House that Mrs Norris monitored the domestic arrangements of the family at the parsonage, finding little to commend and much to criticise, The Reverend Doctor Grant had more of a vocation as a gourmet than as a pastor. Mrs Norris disapproved of Mrs Grant's lavish housekeeping, while Lady Bertram resented that Mrs Grant, with so little beauty, should be so comfortably settled in life. An additional annoyance was that prolonged research by Mrs Norris could only reveal that Doctor Grant's wife had never had more fortune than £5000, £2000 less than the fortune of the Ward sisters.

Doctor Grant, who had met Mrs Norris initially over the delicate question of dilapidations, had increased this offence by refusing to take over the previous incumbent's dining-room table, preferring one of his own, equal in size to that of Mansfield Park. It was not recorded what Mrs Norris did with a table that must have been too big for the White House, but it would be unlikely that she did not find means of usefully adapting it to her more cramped home.

When Sir Thomas sailed for Antigua he knew that the bustling activity of Mrs Norris would provide a counter-balance to the agreeable lethargy in which his wife spent her days, and he had full confidence in the steadiness of his son Edmund. His elder son Sir Thomas took with him, with the idea of detaching Tom from 'bad connections', unspecified, but probably concerned with drinking companions at Newmarket. Tom Bertram was a friend of anyone prepared to share in his amusements.

Lady Bertram supported her husband's departure with fortitude, but his daughters were barely able to conceal their pleasure at the thought of freedom from his control. Sir Thomas had never managed to overcome his pomposity in dealing with Maria and Julia, which they found infinitely less agreeable than the flattery of their Aunt Norris. Fanny would have been prepared to mourn for his going on a dangerous voyage, but she found herself crying because her uncle seemed to think her less improved than he might have hoped. Her cousins put her red eyes down to hypocritical affectation.

The first English caption to the film *Les Visiteurs du Soir* read, 'The Devil sent two of his creatures . . .' and into the castle courtyard Gilles and Dominique (the marvellous Arletty) came riding, beautiful creatures, who bring ruin wherever they appear. Much of this type of disaster was brought about by the arrival at Mansfield Parsonage of Henry and Mary Crawford. They were, presumably, the children of a more prosperous second marriage than that which had produced the poorly dowered Mrs Grant. Henry Crawford had an estate in Norfolk worth £4000 a year, while his sister was known to have a fortune of £20,000.

Although not consciously emissaries of the Devil, Henry and Mary Crawford were an attractive pair, unscrupulous in pursuing their pleasures, and attracting anyone who took their fancy. Additionally, they belonged to a wider world than the county life to which the Miss Bertrams were accustomed. Brought up by their uncle, Admiral Crawford, and his wife, they had been rival pets of a discordant couple. When his wife died, the Admiral, who favoured his nephew, made his niece's position impossible by bringing his mistress to live with him. Mary Crawford, driven to sheltering with her half-sister, was apprehensive of the boredom of country life, but Mrs Grant was delighted to have Mary's company. Doctor Grant liked the stimulation of a pretty girl's presence, and Henry Crawford, as a guest, gave the Doctor an excuse for drinking claret every day.

The Misses Bertram had been presented to local society, but Fanny, the Cinderella, although eighteen, was left at home as companion to Lady Bertram, who would happily fall asleep if read to. Mrs Norris was delighted to chaperone her elder nieces, which left Fanny in undisturbed peace. Besides the pleasure of being driven to local balls at the Bertram's expense, Mrs Norris was prepared to do the scheming for husbands which was beyond the scope of Lady Bertram's temperament. This scheming was so successful that by the date of the arrival of the Crawfords at parsonage, Maria Bertram was as good as engaged to Mr Rushworth of Sotherton Court. He was a man of peculiar dullness, but his recently inherited estate was of imposing magnificence.

Anxious to keep Henry and Mary with her, Mrs Grant first offered the heir, Tom Bertram, as a prospective husband for Mary, and then suggested that Henry might find Julia Bertram an acceptable bride, Maria being already bespoke. Maria had the prospect before her of Mr Rushworth's £12,000 a year, a larger income than her father's. The attraction of Sotherton, 'an ancient manorial residence . . . with all its rights of Court-Leet and Court Baron' was equalled, if not exceeded, by the idea of a house in London. Lady Bertram had long given up going to London with Sir Thomas, when he attended the House of Commons, so Maria was dazzled by the thought of spreading her wings far away from humdrum Northamptonshire. With her future so prosperously settled, it was unlucky that *les visiteurs du soir* had arrived at the parsonage to disturb her in the satisfaction of her choice.

As friendship grew among the young people, it became apparent that, if convenient logic would encourage Henry to fall in love with Julia, it was to Maria that he was attracted. Mary Crawford was prepared to find Tom Bertram agreeable, and indeed she did so, but he was demonstrably more interested in a race in which he had a runner. He left to follow his horse's fortunes. Edmund had none of his brother's conversational rattle, and he had the handicap of being a younger son but, almost against her will, Mary began to find him a more rewarding companion than Tom. When Mr Rushworth tied himself into verbal knots over his proposed alterations to Sotherton, Edmund pulled things together by a judicious assessment that all would be done 'extremely well'. Miss Crawford said to herself, 'He is a well-bred man; he makes the best of it.'

From this base of respect, love built up, watched in calm despair by Fanny. The journey of Miss Crawford's harp to Mansfield Parsonage has been subject for academic jokes, but once it arrived the seduction of Edmund began. He had formed Fanny, not only intellectually, but in her moral judgements. Initially, Edmund and Fanny had agreed that Miss Crawford's mockery of her uncle the Admiral was both ungrateful and in poor taste, but Edmund's disapproval was tinkled away by the notes of the harp, and the picture of its pretty performer, against the backdrop of a summer garden, captivated Edmund. He did, however, have a shock when he found that, taking his mare for Mary to ride, had left Fanny to be slave-driven by Mrs Norris.

Mrs George Austen, mother of Jane, had been born Cassandra Leigh, of the family of Leigh of Stoneleigh Abbey. In 1806, Mrs Austen's cousin, the Reverend Thomas Leigh of Adlestrop, inherited Stoneleigh Abbey, and was warned to take immediate possession of the estate, to assert his rights over other heirs. It happened that Mrs Austen and her daughters, Cassandra and Jane, were staying with their kinsman at Adlestrop, recently 'improved' by Mr Repton. They accompanied the Reverend Thomas Leigh to Stoneleigh. It was an opportunity not wasted on Jane Austen, and provided her with material for one of the great set pieces in *Mansfield Park*.

The misattribution of places in Jane Austen's novels is perhaps at its most extreme in the case of *Pride and Prejudice* which has already been examined. A less well-known misidentification is that of Easton Neston with Mansfield Park, and Stowe with Sotherton. Easton Neston is a magnificent example of the combined art of Christopher Wren and Nicholas Hawksmoor. Although this would be of a far earlier date than 'the modern house' that met with Miss Crawford's approval, in the grounds there is one feature which may possibly have given rise to this misapprehension.

Among the splendid trees in the grounds of Easton Neston, there stands an imposing monument on which the word most easily to be deciphered is PUG. Jane Austen is known to have made inquiries about the landscape of Northamptonshire, so it would not seem impossible that she heard of this 'storied urn', and that the idea of a pug of importance sowed the seed for Lady Bertram's occupation in life. This may be pure speculation, but none the less enjoyable for that. On the other hand, to suggest that Stowe might be the image for Sotherton would pass the bounds of plausibility. The magnificent vistas of Stowe would at once disqualify it as a demesne that needed the improving genius of Mr Repton, or even of the party which set out from Mansfield to Sotherton on a fine summer's day.

Mr Crawford drove his barouche, with Julia sitting on the box beside him. This was an arrangement of Mrs Grant's who persisted in her attempts to allot the youngest Miss Bertram to her brother. In the carriage itself, Mary Crawford, Fanny and Mrs Norris had Maria as their companion. Until they reached the boundary of Mr Rushworth's estate, Maria was tormented by the laughter from her sister at Henry Crawford's jokes. Maria was briefly placated by the sight of her future husband's well-kept property, but even this delectable sight could not check her dangerous flirtation with Henry.

It was in the chapel that something of a showdown took place. Fanny was disappointed at the lack of Gothic solemnity, finding the rich plaster work too much like a drawing-room. What Fanny would have seen, including the red velvet cushions of the family gallery, can be seen at Stoneleigh to this day, but it was the human drama that drew her attention away from contemplating the lack of romance in architecture.

Julia, understandably irked that Maria was not only making a splendid match, but competing for the favour of Mr Crawford, drew attention to Maria and Mr Rushworth as they stood side by side. If only Edmund had taken orders, Julia said, what could be more 'snug' than to celebrate the marriage out of hand? A few minutes before, Miss Crawford had passed some disparaging remarks on the inferior type of man who, contemporaneously, took orders. She was more and more drawn to Edmund, but had not troubled to inform herself as to his destiny. At the realisation that she was getting attached to a prospective clergyman, she could only be described as looking aghast.

The next stage of the afternoon's comedy was played out before Fanny, painfully, when Edmund and Mary left her to rest on a seat. Here she was first joined by Mr Rushworth, Maria and Henry Crawford. After sending off her betrothed to fetch the key into the park, Maria and Henry staged a symbolic elopement by climbing round the gate and walking away in the opposite direction to that suggested by Mr Rushworth. Before they left Fanny, their conversation had made her increasingly uncomfortable, passing beyond the exchange of light flirtation. Shortly afterwards, Fanny was joined by Julia in a furious temper, having had to support the burden of old Mrs Rushworth's prosings. Julia, in here turn, scrambled round the gate, and set off in pursuit of Maria and Henry. The comedy turned to farce, when Mr Rushworth joined Fanny, deeply disgusted that his guests had not had the good manners to wait for him.

Fanny put forward what soothing excuses she could evolve, but when Mr Rushworth began to criticise Henry Crawford, she could only agree silently. Mr Rushworth thought that no one could honestly consider the undersized Mr Crawford handsome. 'He is not five foot nine. I should not wonder if he was not more than five foot eight.' (Mr Rushworth, it might be deduced, would appear to have measured six foot) Even more could Fanny agree with her host's sentiment that local society had got on very well without the Crawfords. Regarded by Edmund as a dull fellow, redeemed by £12,000 a year, Mr Rushworth could, at least, recognise an enemy.

In fairness to Mrs Norris, she was prepared to admire frugality in others with disinterested generosity. On the drive home, laden with spoils from Sotherton, she assured Maria of the excellent domestic economy practised by the housekeeper at Maria's future home. As Maria's chief object in marrying Mr Rushworth was to spend his fortune, she may have been far from pleased at the idea of a housekeeper remarkable for thriftiness, though this had been no barrier to Mrs Norris from 'spunging' a cream-cheese, a sitting of pheasants' eggs, and a rare variety of heath.

Jane Austen was well aware that the first fortnight in September would be dedicated to partridge-shooting by every country landowner. Tom Bertram, in consequence, returned to Mansfield, while Henry Crawford went to deal with his own partridges in Norfolk. He left a depressing gap in the day-to-day life of the Misses Bertram. Meanwhile, Mr Rushworth's long stories to Maria of his own feats against wild birds, and still wilder poachers, gave her an unpalatable foretaste of what his conversation after marriage would be.

It was not only the importance of partridges that Jane Austen understood and used creatively in her plots. She was an adept at handling the domino effect that a distant event might have on the lives of her principal characters. The death of a dowager grandmother, at a great distance, obliged the punctilious Lord Ravenshaw to abandon some theatricals, and to break up the company gathered to perform in them. Consequently, the Honourable John Yates, the rather unsatisfactory son of another peer, was suddenly thrown on the world. He then took advantage of an open invitation to Mansfield Park, given shortly before by his new best friend, Tom Bertram.

Mr Yates' complaint at the cancellation of the performance of *Lovers' Vows*, and his description of the dramatic excitement that had been lost, infected Tom and his sisters. It was decided that a play must be produced at Mansfield, where Sir Thomas was not expected to return until November. The intervening weeks would, it might be said, give the mice a last opportunity to play before the cat reappeared to call them to order, and re-impose his customary restrictions.

It was easier to set up a theatre than to decide on a play. Tom pronounced the billiard table to be 'vile', but discovered that if it was banished the room would make an excellent playhouse. The opening of a door into Sir Thomas' business room, his favourite apartment, would provide a green room with an entrance on to the stage. Being at the back of the house, the billiard room, and Sir Thomas' room adjoining, were out of earshot from events in the front hall.

Ever an imaginative editor, Doctor Chapman supplied the script of *Lovers' Vows*, (translated from the German of Kotzebue, by Mrs Inchbald, performed at the Theatre Royal Covent Garden in 1798). He pointed out that this was an almost essential Appendix for any reader who wished to understand the development of *Mansfield Park*. Few plays can stand up to a cold-blooded analysis of the plot, and *Lovers'*

Vows tottered on the edge of absurdity. The two leading characters, Agatha and Frederick, her natural son by Baron Wildenheim, had passionate scenes together which could only suggest a conscious Oedipus and Jocasta. Maria Bertram and Henry Crawford, who took the parts, made good use of every opportunity to intensify their flirtation.

The love affair had become so blatant, that Julia Bertram had ceased to strive for Henry Crawford's attention, spurning his last efforts to placate her. Mr Rushworth had been given the part of Count Cassel, a foppish character for whom Mrs Norris was commissioned to make a pink satin cloak. In addition, Mrs Norris was concerned with a green baize curtain. Lady Bertram remained seated beside her pug, with a vague idea that she might attend a rehearsal when she was more at leisure.

Edmund had failed to persuade Tom and Maria that the play would certainly be regarded by their father as a gross impropriety, but he had held out against acting himself. With all the inconsistency of love, however, when Miss Crawford agreed to take the part of Amelia, the second female lead, he could not resist the fascination. Fanny suffered more from this illogicality than Edmund himself. He found the excuse that otherwise Tom would recruit any strange young man to take the part of Amelia's lover. Fanny was well aware that this was yet a further example of Miss Crawford's power over the cousin who held her heart.

Julia Bertram had set up a rival flirtation with Mr Yates, but would not have dreamt of making Fanny her companion in crossed love. Yates, himself, gave his full voice to the part of Baron Waldenheim, while Agatha (Maria) and Frederick (Henry) perfected their

rôles in such privacy as they could find. Miss Crawford, adept at oiling social wheels, assured Mr Rushworth how excellently *maternal* was Maria's acting,
but even his dull mind felt that something sinister
was building up. Fanny had the heavy task of trying
to teach Mr Rushworth the two and forty speeches
assigned to Count Cassel.

Eventually matters progressed so far that a
rehearsal of the first three acts could be undertaken.
All the players were assembled in the billiard-room
theatre, with Fanny conscripted to read a minor part,
when Jane Austen exploded the most dramatic of her
bombshells. The noise of the rehearsal had blotted
out all other sounds from the house, when Julia burst
into the room, her face all aghast. (I. Compton-
Burnett quoted Julia's speech at an analogous scene
in *A House and its Head*.)

'[Julia] exclaimed, "My father is come! He is in the
hall at this moment." '

At a later stage in the novel, Henry Crawford
described Shakespeare 'as part of an Englishman's
constitution'. When Julia burst upon the rehearsal
with her devastating news, she was at once disgusted
to see that Henry continued to press Maria's hand to
his heart. Angrily, she retreated, with the acid remark
that she, at least, had no need to fear her father's
appearance. With his respect for Shakespeare, Henry
must surely have remembered the bastard Edmund's
speech in *King Lear*, 'To both these sisters have I
sworn my love, Each jealous of the other as the stung
are of the adder.' But he continued to press Agatha/
Maria's hand to his heart, although the tale of her
seduction which had led to his (Frederick's) birth had
been so violently interrupted.

Feeling only too like mice to whom the cat had

made an unseasonably early return, his family went to greet Sir Thomas. With the exception of Mr Yates, all knew that the show would not go on, depriving the expectant neighbourhood of a dramatic treat. Maria had the additional agitation of hoping that the hand, so recently pressed to Henry Crawford's heart, might be claimed by him as that of his future wife.

Mr Yates continued to rehearse, solo, at the top of his voice, and this hallooing startled Sir Thomas when he entered 'his own dear room'. Stepping into the billiard room he was even more astonished to find himself among the confused trappings of a theatre. Although only too aware of his father's impending displeasure, Tom Bertram, following, had difficulty in suppressing his helpless laughter at the tremendous start Yates gave at the sight of Tom's father. The unrehearsed effect was of the highest quality. As Jane Austen wrote, 'the house would close with the greatest éclat.'

Although devoid of the power of self-criticism, Mrs Norris was sensitive to storm signals. Some instinct warned her to conceal from Sir Thomas' sight the pink satin cloak that was to compensate Mr Rushworth for his minor part in *Lovers' Vows*. Its eventual fate remained unknown, but the green baize curtain accompanied Mrs Norris across the park to her cottage, where she happened to have a particular need for green baize.

When Sir Thomas attempted to suggest to his sister-in-law that she might have prevented the theatrical enterprise taking such an extravagant form, Mrs Norris talked him down so volubly that he gave up in despair, hopeless of making her express any regret. Mrs Norris, herself, took refuge in proclaiming the skill with which she had manoeuvred the match between Maria and Mr Rushworth.

On Maria's side, hopes that she would be claimed by Henry Crawford, and that Mr Rushworth could be discarded, were dashed within a few hours of Sir Thomas' arrival. Henry left for Bath with no promise of returning, except in the event of *Lovers' Vows* being resumed, which all knew to be an impossibility. After the first shock of being ruthlessly deserted, Maria determined to hasten her marriage, which would, at least, show Mr Crawford that, if he had stolen her heart, he had not blocked her worldly progress.

Lack of feeling, even of tolerance, for Mr Rushworth was the chief obstacle in Maria's path. This became so blatant that Sir Thomas remarked upon it, and even offered to extract Maria from her engagement. She, however, rebuffed her father, and resolved to be more circumspect in her behaviour to her betrothed. Wishing to believe Maria's assertion that Mr Rushworth would make her happy, Sir Thomas gave his daughter away without extreme misgiving. Mrs Norris, in the triumph of her scheming, drank the couple's health in a few extra glasses. She would not seem to have passed out, but it could be speculated that her parsimony financed a habit of secret drinking, which would also account for her bursts of bad temper.

Henry Crawford's triflings had caused fierce rivalry between the sisters, but his defection brought them together. No longer needing to be jealous of Maria, 'as the stung are of the adder', Julia was as glad to accompany her sister to Brighton on her honeymoon, as was Maria to be spared a tête-à-tête with Mr Rushworth. This unfortunate man was, it is to be hoped, too obtuse to notice that he was escorting two broken hearts along the Chain Pier.

The departure of the two sisters, far from ugly though they were, marked the beginning of Fanny's emergence from the chrysalis of a Cinderella into the butterfly of a princess. On returning from his voyage, Sir Thomas had greeted her with more affection than he had ever shown before, and Edmund assured him of the rightness of Fanny's behaviour during the theatricals. In return, Sir Thomas expressed his pleasure in Fanny's newly developed prettiness. Sir Thomas did not actually fall in love with Fanny, but he was obviously attracted to her. Had Lady Bertram sunk into a doze from which she did not wake, Fanny might have found herself in the painful position of refusing Edmund's father, the Table of Kindred and Affinity neglecting to forbid a marriage with the (widowed) husband of an aunt.

Mrs Norris still remained unwilling to cease her suppression of Fanny. An invitation to dine at the parsonage with Doctor and Mrs Grant gave her Aunt Norris an opportunity to lecture Fanny on taking the lowliest place, and to insist, however wet the evening, that she must be prepared to walk home. When Sir Thomas ordered the carriage for his niece, Mrs Norris could hardly contain her rage.

Fanny's dress, white with glossy spots, had been given her by Sir Thomas for Maria's wedding, and was admired by Edmund. The cousins drove up the parsonage to find that a Prince, if a heartless one, had arrived. Secure in the knowledge that Maria and Julia had left for Brighton, Henry Crawford had returned with his hunters to the parsonage. Crawford was incapable of refraining from loosing his charm on any woman who came his way. Fanny's coldness of behaviour when he talked of the sad cancellation of *Lovers' Vows* was exactly the challenge needed to excite his interest. His compliments fell flat before Fanny's disapproval. By the following morning, Henry Crawford had decided that he would enliven non-hunting days by making Fanny Price fall in love with him.

Mary Crawford protested that, though a little love might animate Fanny, the poor girl should not be exposed to the full force of Henry's charm, but her brother said, with some truth, that this would only be the affair of a fortnight, and if that could kill Fanny nothing could save her. All he asked was smiles as well as blushes, a chair kept for him by Fanny's side, an interest in all his possessions and pleasures, and, failing to detain him at Mansfield, the feeling, at his departure, that she would never be happy again. 'Moderation itself!' said Mary, but she left Fanny to her fate.

Protected by her love for another, Fanny was steeled against advances which she knew from observation to be based on self-indulgent fickleness. Accustomed to a too eager response from girls who understood flirtation, Henry's perseverance led him to fall in love with Fanny himself, while she remained aloof. The arrival of William Price, the midshipman, gave Henry an insight into the warmth of feeling that Fanny possessed, and could bestow even on a brother. Dalliance was transformed into a determination to marry Fanny, and Mary Crawford, more than half in love with Edmund, welcomed the connection. Even Sir Thomas recognised that a less lofty mind than his would have said that Mr Crawford was courting Miss Price.

It was in *Mansfield Park* that three of Jane Austen's

own brothers made what might be called guest appearances, rather as dolphins flash out of the waves and submerge again. The simile is not inappropriate, as it was her sailor brothers, Frank and Charles, who provided material for her portrait of William Price. She did not, however, give either of their names to Fanny's brother. Henry Austen, on the other hand, had besides the Christian name many of the characteristics which his sister Jane gave to Henry Crawford, but not, unfortunately, 'his pretty estate' in Norfolk of £4000 a year.

When she came to create the wholly delightful William Price, Jane Austen chipped pieces off both Charles and Frank. When Charles had some prize money in his pocket he bought topaz crosses, which survive to this day, for his sisters Cassandra and Jane ('He must be well scolded,' Jane wrote). Similarly, William Price bought a Maltese cross for Fanny. This cross played a part in Henry Crawford's courtship. With a characteristic mixture of duplicity and good nature, Henry bought a chain on which to hang William's gift, and deluded Fanny into accepting it as a present from Mary. It was Frank's promotion to lieutenant that brought a whoop of joy from his sister Jane. 'Frank is made,' she exclaimed in a letter. William Price's promotion was engineered by Henry Crawford in an appeal to his uncle the Admiral. This was yet another step in Henry's plot to drive Fanny into a corner from which her only escape would be to accept his proposal.

Henry Crawford's career as a smart young man about town, with means to support a life of pleasure, had taught him to believe himself irresistible to any woman he wished to please. He had had no doubts that he could make Fanny fall in love with him. If he believed that she was aware of his recent Goneril and Regan situation with her cousins, he probably imagined that such a down-trodden poor relation would relish capturing a prize that had eluded Maria and Julia. When he proposed he had no doubt that he would be accepted with the gentle modesty that he valued in her character. With, as it were, her brother William's promotion to second lieutenant on board HMS *Thrush* in his hand, how could Fanny refuse Henry?

Fanny's refusal, a stone cast into the calm pool of life at Mansfield Park, sent ripples through both the Park and the parsonage. Sir Thomas was astounded, and, in an interview in the old schoolroom, Fanny's refuge, reduced his niece to tears. In fairness to Sir Thomas, when he found that, by a ruling of Mrs Norris, Fanny had no fire in her sitting room, he immediately ordered one to be lit. He even made a sort of apology for Mrs Norris' suppression of Fanny, adding that should Fanny's fortunes improve, he trusted that she would not treat her aunt with less respect.

By refusing Mr Crawford, Fanny was as much alone among persecutors as a young virgin in hell, on a church porch in the Middle Ages. Henry might be expected to be taken aback, and Mary Crawford to be disappointed, but Fanny had also to contend with the uncomprehending surprise of her dear brother William, and her even dearer cousin Edmund. The latter was particularly obtuse, brushing aside Fanny's representation of Crawford's unprincipled behaviour at the time of the theatricals. It was a measure of the general disregard of Fanny's feelings at Mansfield, that no one had noticed that her devotion to Edmund went beyond cousinly grati-

tude for his kindness. His fancy for Miss Crawford
acted as smoke screen, behind which Fanny sheltered.
Even Sir Thomas, who had apprehended cousins in
love as a danger in adopting Fanny, was deceived by
the composure learnt in her days of subservience.

Lady Bertram offered her niece a solitary piece of
advice, on hearing of Henry Crawford's proposal.
She had treated Fanny as a slave to her everyday
round of carpet work and tea-making, but she had
never bestirred herself to suggest any course of
behaviour. Now she told Fanny that it was the duty
of every young woman to accept the offer of an
eligible young man. She even made a greater effort
of encouragement, promising Fanny a puppy when
pug had a litter. Eight years before, when Fanny was
first expected at Mansfield Park, Lady Bertram had
hoped that Fanny would not tease her poor pug,
because she had 'just got Julia to leave it alone'. Lady
Bertram's pugs were, obviously, a dynasty, in this
earliest mention with no declared sex.

In the hot summer, the background of the assorted
dramas which convulsed the household, Lady
Bertram spoke of the exhaustion of a morning spent
calling pug, definitely a male, off the flower beds.
The excitement of Sir Thomas' return even caused
her to move Pug (with a capital) to make room
for her husband on her sofa. Somewhere, in the six
months between mid-summer and the following
January, Lady Bertram must have changed a dog pug
for a bitch, from whom she certainly expected a
litter.

Sir Thomas' reaction to what he considered to
be Fanny's obduracy was to give her a taste of the
discomforts from which she had been plucked as a
child of ten years old. Under the escort of the newly

made Lieutenant Price, it was arranged for her to pay a visit to Portsmouth, and to see the family to whom she had been so long a stranger. Fanny was in ecstasies at the idea of returning to her mother, and being valued, on equal terms, by her brothers and sisters. After some agonised moments when Mrs Norris threatened to make a third in the post chaise, Fanny and William set off happily on a journey paid for by Sir Thomas. Mrs Norris had realised that, though she could get a free ride to see 'her poor dear sister Price', she would be obliged to pay for her own journey back to Mansfield.

As a culture shock, Sir Thomas' dispatch of Fanny to Portsmouth was almost too great a success. She found herself in a dirty house, full of unpleasant smells and bursting with children. Her parents were to be no consolation. Her mother was a domestic incompetent, only interested in her sons, except for an injudicious spoiling of Betsy, her youngest, goddaughter of Mrs Norris, whose name may be deduced to have been Elizabeth. Fanny's hopes of being a valued daughter to a loving parent evaporated. She had had little expectation of finding a father sympathetic to the refinements of her upbringing, but the reality was worse than she had feared.

When Mr Price, Lieutenant of Marines (Ret) walked into the house to which his eldest, long absent daughter had just returned, he found the luggage of his son and daughter impeding his passage. These he kicked aside with an oath, and, calling for a candle which was not brought, made his way into the parlour. Mr Price, an Hogarthian character, strangely neglected by serious students of the novels, greeted his son William with warmth, and described HMS *Thrush* going out of harbour with an almost poetical fervour. When Fanny was brought to his notice, he gave her a cordial hug, and supposed that she would soon want a husband. Mr Price was clearly not a worrying type. The continuous stream of babies that had increased the squalor of his home had done nothing to make him feel that matrimony was not the destiny of any pretty young woman.

Further experience of her father did nothing to reconcile Fanny to what might be called, in America, his 'personality defects'. Mr Price drank, he also swore and shaved only for Sundays. His chief notice of Fanny, rather priggishly educated by her cousin Edmund, was to make her the subject of embarrassingly coarse jokes. Bullied she may have been at Mansfield Park, but there she was, at least, taken seriously. Her refusal of Mr Crawford's eligible proposals had agitated the household, from her uncle and aunts to Baddeley the butler. At Portsmouth, she had to bear with an unshaven father, who read only the newspaper (this habit was to supply a key to the book's plot) and the Navy List. Mr Price's life as an amateur tide watcher, however, gave him an occupation satisfying to himself.

More trying to Fanny than the discomforts of her old home, was the apprehension that any post might bring a letter announcing that Edmund had been accepted by Miss Crawford. This torture was prolonged by a letter from the egregious Edmund, who had, in London, been discouraged by Mary's circle of worldly friends, and had not put his fate to the touch.

In the meantime, Henry Crawford appeared at Portsmouth, and his exposure to the chaos of her parents' house threw Fanny into an agony. It was a Saturday, and her father's bristly chin was a harsh

contrast to the elegance of her admirer. Henry Crawford behaved impeccably, and as an emissary from
what she now regarded as her home, Fanny found
him improved in gentleness. She could not delude
herself that his love might not fade, but, naturally,
she would prefer that this should be caused by her
persistent refusals, rather than by disgust at the inferi-
ority of her family circumstances.

The news that Tom Bertram had returned home
after what seems to have been an attack of pneumonia, which threatened to damage his lungs,
brought Fanny a letter from Miss Crawford. The
letter showed that charming girl in a most unattractive light. If Tom succumbed, and Edmund became
his father's heir, Mary would be prepared to overlook
what she regarded as his premature taking of Holy
Orders. Besides this display of worldly calculation,
Mary found it necessary to tell Fanny that Henry's
devotion was unfaltering, although he had been staying at Richmond, only a ferry ride across the Thames
from Twickenham, where Mrs Rushworth was visiting friends.

It was hard to say which of these comments disgusted Fanny most, being awkwardly placed as a
confidant of Edmund, and, reluctantly, of Mary. She
had thought to observe improvement in Henry, and
she now found that a chilliness in Mrs Rushworth's
manner had caused him to renew his blandishments.
Fanny had not had the experience to have learnt that
to a Lothario such as Henry Crawford, no victim,
however long abandoned, could be allowed, perma-
nently, to escape.

The next note from Miss Crawford was both agitated and enigmatic. It appeared that gossip was
going round London concerning the departure of

Mrs Rushworth from her husband's house, and linking her name with that of Henry Crawford. Baffled, but with all her initial distrust of Henry renewed, Fanny could only accept Mary's rather wild assurances that Henry was escorting Maria and Julia to Mansfield Park.

Enlightenment came from a most unexpected source. While Fanny brooded over the mystery, her father, as was his custom, read the newspaper with close attention, before returning it to a neighbour. Suddenly he inquired of what was the name of her grand cousins in Wimpole Street. When she said 'Rushworth' Mr Price showed her a paragraph in his newspaper which deeply regretted to inform its readers that Mrs R., newly married, and a promising hostess, had left her husband's roof in the company of the captivating Mr C., and even the editor did not know of their destination.

The only word to describe Mr Price's sentiments would be *schadenfreude*. He cheerfully suggested that flogging with a rope's end for both parties would be his treatment for such behaviour, adding, with a sneer, that Sir Thomas might be too much of a fine gentleman to object to his daughter's adultery. Fanny worried herself into a state of near collapse, before she was raised into euphoria by the news that Edmund would be arriving at once to take her, and her sister Susan, back to Mansfield Park. To find herself rescued from Portsmouth, and allowed to take Susan with her, was a double cause of rejoicing. Susan had struggled with impossible domestic conditions, and to bring her to the civilisation of Mansfield would have been a pleasure. It was however, almost lost in the ecstasy of a heart, long prepared for immolation, but which now knew that Edmund must be released from the thrall of Miss Crawford.

Fanny's departure from her father's house was as confused and devoid of refreshment as her arrival had been. Edmund had already told her that his sister Julia, appalled by the prospect of the restrictions at home that Maria's elopement would inflict on her, had taken the remedy nearest to hand. She had gone to Scotland with the Honourable John Yates, and, unlike Lydia Bennet (*Pride and Prejudice*) she had actually crossed the border to a land where a declaration of marriage before any two witnesses was valid.

This elopement was a very minor sensation. Fanny was more concerned with the ravages his disappointment might have inflicted on Edmund. He, on the other hand, attributed Fanny's wan looks to the blow that Crawford's betrayal had given to her growing regard. Edmund's habit of misinterpreting Fanny's state of mind and body was, on this occasion, excusable. He did not know that her health had suffered from an inability to eat the unpalatable meals set before her at Portsmouth, and that she had largely subsisted on buns and biscuits brought in by her younger brothers.

At Mansfield, Fanny found her Aunt Bertram touchingly glad to see her, while her Aunt Norris, though cowed, retained some power of being disagreeable. She blamed Fanny for causing the débâcle by refusing Mr Crawford. Otherwise Mrs Norris had hardly enough spirit left to condemn Susan as yet another indigent niece. Of the rest of the family, Tom was sobered up by his illness, and became more of a comfort to his father than could, at one time, have been expected. The Honourable Mrs Yates was anxious to be taken back into the family, and her husband turned out to be less of an extreme detrimental than had sometimes appeared likely.

Maria's fate was harsher. Divorced by Mr Rushworth, and failing to persuade Henry Crawford to marry her, as his sister had shocked Edmund by suggesting, she was condemned to live sequestered with only Mrs Norris as her companion. In her letters, Jane Austen made some tart comments on an adulteress she had picked out in a gathering at Bath. This Miss Twisleton, having been divorced for criminal conversation, as was Maria Bertram, had reverted to her maiden name. Miss Twisleton's sister was married to James Leigh, cousin of Mrs Austen, whose daughter Jane thoroughly disapproved of this branch of the family. Miss Twisleton lived a far from sequestered life, and subsequently remarried. Jane Austen allowed no such rehabilitation to Maria Bertram.

Even when her noblest characters were on the point of having their difficulties resolved, Jane Austen could seldom resist an affectionately deflating comment. It took Edmund three days after the return to Mansfield before he could bring himself to tell Fanny of his final interview with Miss Crawford. Edmund's conversation was habitually priggish, but on this occasion he let rip his feelings. Miss Crawford had appalled him by her pragmatic approach to her brother's elopement with Maria, declaring that the only way out of the imbroglio would be for a marriage between the guilty parties. Edmund's shocked reaction startled Mary, though she made an attempt to seduce him from leaving her in disgust at her attitude.

With an air of resolution that momentarily deceived Fanny, Edmund declared that he would not again trouble her on the subject. But, as Jane Austen pointed out, Edmund's distress was too acute for him to arrive at such a closure. Together with Fanny, he discussed Mary's many good qualities, admirable if her mind had not been poisoned by worldly friends.

It was then that Fanny, previously playing her hand with her cards close to her chest, led out a small but significant trump. She revealed to Edmund that Miss Crawford's increasing regard for Edmund had resulted from the expectation that Tom Bertram was likely to succumb from an attack on his lungs, leaving his brother heir to Mansfield Park. Not unnaturally, Edmund resisted the idea, but when he came to accept this evidence of deepest worldliness, it was another step in his disenchantment. Once he had agreed that Miss Crawford was a calculating minx, Fanny was quite prepared to settle with Edmund that no other woman could ever take possession of his heart.

One of Sir Thomas' original objections to adopting Fanny had been the fear of cousins falling in love. This idea had been pooh-poohed by Mrs Norris. She declared that it would be far more likely that a generous young man, first meeting a beggar maid of a cousin at a marriageable age, would be bewitched. This opinion did appear to be well-founded, in that Edmund was obviously attracted to Mary Crawford. That she had no longer to listen to rhapsodies on Miss Crawford's perfections was, for the present, enough to content Fanny.

An added pleasure was the departure of Mrs Norris to set up an establishment with Maria. Sir Thomas was among those thankful for her disappearance, having come to realise that her influence on his family had been injudicious, if not positively malign. Mrs

Norris was given no credit by Jane Austen for following her favourite Maria into a seclusion predicted as likely to be bad-tempered. The most allowed for a virtue in Mrs Norris was that she would have been a more respectable mother of nine children on a small income than her incompetent sister Price, though the latter might well have made as good a fine lady as her sister Bertram.

Sir Thomas was soon to be in the position of promoting the very marriage between his son Edmund and his niece Fanny, 'cousins in Love', which he had once feared. Edmund's discovery that he loved Fanny was greeted with enthusiasm by his father, whose own weakness for his niece became ever more pronounced. Fanny could, at last, admit that her heart had belonged to Edmund for many a weary year. With a touch of inimitable slyness, Jane Austen left it to the reader to decide the span of time before Edmund could recover from the loss of Miss Crawford.

The awkwardness of the Grants, who had brought *les visiteurs du soir* to Mansfield, continuing as near neighbours was obviated by Doctor Grant unexpectedly being appointed to a stall in Westminster. Fanny and Edmund, having married, had set up house in Edmund's living of Thornton Lacy. They could now transfer to the parsonage at Mansfield, where Fanny had passed so many uneasy hours. Fortunately, Mrs Norris was now at a sufficient distance for her comments to be unheard.

Not only had Sir Thomas' original benevolence given him an ideal daughter in Fanny, his help in settling the rest of the Price family in suitable careers was rewarded by the successes they achieved. Jane Austen attributed this, in part, to the discipline of early hardship. She did not add, what might be thought to be an inescapable conclusion, that among the handicaps overcome was that of a father whose main occupation was the study of gossip columns, while he tippled rum and water.

4

Emma

'OH, MISS WOODHOUSE, HOW YOU DO
FORGET.'

Sometime about the year 1920, Eton boys, at a certain level in the school, were given Jane Austen's
Emma to read as a holiday task. This would have
been in the Christmas holidays, and my mother, with
a son whose taste for literature was undeveloped,
decided to read the book aloud to her assembled
family. She felt that this would, at least, ensure that
the tide of *Emma* had flowed over him, even if it
receded without leaving much in the way of drift-
wood in his memory. The rest of the family listened
with appreciation, including myself, an eight-year-
old daughter. In my memory was fixed the chivalry
of Mr Weston in borrowing two umbrellas, to shelter
Emma, and Miss Taylor, his future wife, and the
gallantry of Robert Martin in making a special journey to procure walnuts for Harriet Smith. This
initiation culminated in a devotion to Jane Austen
which has led to the building of this compendium.
    To Jane Austen the beginning of a novel led,
inexorably, to the unwinding of a plot. Some event,

unexpected and not always welcome, shook the kaleidoscope, and caused a new pattern to emerge. The event had no need to be highly dramatic. Nothing could have been quieter than the marriage of Miss Taylor, formerly Emma's governess, latterly more of a companion, to Mr Weston, which was the opening of the novel. The marriage did, however, leave Emma herself with no friend in the house to whom she could talk on equal terms. Her father had his life as a valetudinarian to occupy his limited wits. Emma cherished Mr Woodhouse, but Miss Taylor's marriage had left her bereft.

By endowing Emma with an invalidish, or rather hypochondriac, father, Jane Austen was able to limit the Woodhouses' social circle, making Emma to be a large fish in a small pool. Hartfield, her father's house, was the most imposing in Highbury, a cheerful town, but not much given to fashionable life. It was from this narrow sphere that Mr Woodhouse's evening companions at cards were drawn. Dinner was at four o'clock, but as dinner guests made Mr Woodhouse nervous, it would be about six o'clock that the carriage was sent to fetch the three regular guests. These ladies, Mrs Bates, aged widow of a former rector, Miss Bates, her good-natured chattering daughter, and Mrs Goddard, headmistress of a select boarding school for girls, made up a table to which Mr Woodhouse was happily accustomed.

The evening would end with a supper, minced chicken, scalloped oysters, boiled eggs and custard. This was served to the company, while Mr Woodhouse was apt to limit his meal to a dish of gruel, thin, but not too thin. He warned the company against the custard, from which it might be speculated that Mr Woodhouse suffered from a form of acidosis. He did, however, allow that a small egg, boiled as only Serle, the Hartfield cook, knew how, might not be unwholesome.

It was Mrs Goddard, the schoolmistress, who introduced Harriet Smith into Hartfield, an introduction which appeared at first to fill the gap left in Emma's life by the defection into matrimony of Mrs Weston. Harriet Smith, a parlour boarder at Mrs Goddard's school, was the natural daughter of someone unknown to herself. Mrs Goddard's school was the only family she knew. Pretty, fair, plump, she was the exact opposite to the elegant hazel-eyed Emma. To gain such an unquestioning admirer was a great lift to Miss Woodhouse's spirits. She could not foresee that Harriet, innocently dim-witted, was to be the cause of her benefactress making a fool of herself, and even to become a threat to Emma's own happiness.

It was always a pleasure to Jane Austen to have a small laugh at Emma's expense. She did so when describing Emma's first step in supposedly useful friendship towards Harriet Smith. This was to endeavour to find out who might be Harriet's parents. In this Emma failed. Harriet proved to be deplorably lacking in the active curiosity by which, Emma believed, she would herself have unravelled the truth. Miss Woodhouse had her own system for establishing facts. She was capable of making an assertion, based on a surmise, and then quickly elevate the assertion into an article of faith. Having picked out Harriet as a companion, the natural corollary was to decide that she must be the daughter of a gentleman. Consequently, Emma insisted that Harriet should be particularly careful to preserve her station, in a world all too ready to sneer at bastardy.

On her marriage, Mrs Weston had acquired not only a husband but a stepson, fruit of Mr Weston's first marriage to Miss Churchill of Enscombe. Although this marriage had not caused such a complete rupture with the bride's family as that of Miss Frances Ward to Lieutenant Price, RM, the Churchill pride brought about a degree of alienation, only cured by the death of the first Mrs Weston.

The reconciliation took the form of Mr and Mrs Churchill adopting little Master Weston, and turning him into Frank Churchill. It has been said, in considering *Mansfield Park*, that Jane Austen knew about the mechanics of adoption, but there is no evidence that the Knight family of Chawton and Godmersham, the adoptive parents of Edward Austen, behaved with the mixture of spoiling and tyranny which kept Frank Churchill on a short rein. Mrs Churchill was the principal agent in this cat-and-mouse game. Puffed up by her grand marriage, she dominated her husband and adopted son by a parade of ill-health of a far more active kind than Mr Woodhouse's mild invalidism. On his father's remarriage all Highbury judged that it would be correct for Frank Churchill to visit his father, and pay his compliments to his stepmother.

This prospective visit was looked forward to by Emma with what Jane Austen might have called 'a consciousness'. Fully aware of the pleasures of ruling her father's house with a liberty that marriage might curtail, Emma had an idea that, should she make up her mind to marry, Frank Churchill would be a possible husband. She had more than a suspicion that the Westons themselves hoped for such a development. The only obstacle which prevented the young people from getting to know each other was the persistent failure of Frank Churchill to visit Randalls, his father's house.

When Mrs Woodhouse died, she had left her husband with two daughters, Emma, and an older sister, Isabella, who inherited some of her father's characteristics. By nature plaintive, Isabella was in a perpetual dither about the health of those she loved. These increased rapidly in number after her marriage to Mr John Knightley, a lawyer rising in his profession, but with no love for society. His elder brother, George, was the owner of Donwell Abbey, and of the largest estate in the neighbourhood. This connection had resulted in George Knightley becoming a close friend of Emma, and a frequent caller at Hartfield, where he treated Mr Woodhouse's fancies with kindness, but clashed with Emma over what he regarded as her misplaced stratagems.

A stratagem which aroused protest in Mr Knightley at the beginning of the novel was Emma's idea of finding a wife for the Reverend Mr Elton, incumbent of the parish of Highbury. Inevitably, the bride chosen by Emma was her protégée, Harriet Smith, and she set to work to convince Harriet that Mr Elton was well on the way to falling in love with her. First of all it was necessary to detach Harriet's thoughts from Robert Martin, a young farmer of exemplary character, but thought by Emma to be beneath her notice socially, and too prosperous to need Emma's charitable help. Harriet had been staying with the Martins when her host had made a special journey to find walnuts for Miss Smith.

Isolated by her father's dislike of strange faces, and predilection for quiet card-parties among old friends, Emma had no rivals for her position at the head of Highbury's social ladder. She wished, in consequence to rescue Harriet from sinking to be the wife of Robert Martin of Abbey Farm. When Mr Martin actually wrote proposing to Harriet, Emma had to use a good deal of cunning in manoeuvring her little friend into refusing the offer. It was only when Harriet announced a reluctant intention of turning down Mr Martin, that Emma revealed the impossibility of keeping Mrs Martin of Abbey Farm on her visiting list. The narrowness of her escape from a future unvisited by Miss Woodhouse went some way to cheer Harriet from the depression caused by paining an admirer to whom she was undeniably partial.

Emma's satisfaction in averting this danger to Harriet was badly shaken when Mr Knightley appeared, and expected her to be pleased at the news of Robert Martin's proposal to Harriet. Mr Knightley had never approved of Harriet's intimacy at Hartfield, judging her to be an ignorant flatterer, who would encourage Emma in self-conceit. Arguing that Emma had deprived Harriet of an excellently suitable match, he also warned her, though she paid little heed to warnings, that, had she Mr Elton in mind for Harriet, she would be barking up the wrong tree.

In spite of warnings from Mr Knightley, Emma continued to impress on Harriet that Mr Elton was in love with her. Harriet's small brain was exercised on making a collection of riddles and charades. She had already transcribed a 'well-known charade' when Mr Elton offered it, but he did so with so much sentiment that Emma regretted the discouragement of telling him he was forestalled.

The charade ran:

> My first doth affliction denote,
> Which my second is destined to feel,

And my whole is the best antidote,
That affliction to soften and heal.

Wo(e)man was the solution, which Jane Austen left
the reader to guess.

Mr Elton, whose egregiousness became ever more
apparent, also produced a riddle in three verses, of
which the solution was Courtship. To this two lines
were added:

Thy ready wit the word will soon supply,
May its approval beam in that soft eye.

Although she felt that ready wit was hardly a quality
of Harriet's, Emma persisted in her conviction that
this was a prelude to a declaration of love, whose
blindness would account for allotting such wit to
Harriet.

The Christmas visit of the John Knightleys, and
their five children, slowed down Emma's match-
making, but an outing to dine at Randalls, on Christmas Eve, gave Miss Woodhouse a disagreeable
shock. She had brushed aside a brotherly warning
from John Knightley that Mr Elton appeared to be
making up to Emma herself. As Harriet was in bed
with a bad sore throat, Emma had assured Mr Elton
that he had every reason to excuse himself from the
Westons' dinner party. Christmas Day was, after all,
a strenuous feast for a clergyman. It was Mr Elton's
archly gallant thanks for Emma's concern that promoted John Knightley's warning to watch her step.

Snow fell during the dinner party at Randalls,
giving John Knightley the opportunity for some
heartless teasing of his father-in-law. In the hurry to
drive back to Hartfield, Emma found herself alone

in a carriage with Mr Elton. He at once seized her hand, with professions of devotion which he felt confident would not be disagreeable to her. Emma fought a rear-guard action on behalf of Harriet, only to receive a contemptuous dismissal of Miss Smith as a match beneath him. He felt he might look higher than a girl of unknown parentage.

Insulted as she was by Mr Elton's contempt for Harriet, Emma was even angrier that he should consider himself, an upstart nobody, to be an aspirant for the hand of Miss Woodhouse of Hartfield. In the short carriage drive to the vicarage, both parties were in such a furious temper, that, as Jane Austen so wonderfully wrote, 'their straightforward emotions left no room for the little zig-zags of embarrassment'. It would be right, before leaving this crisis, to mention that Emma suspected Mr Elton to have drunk too much of 'Mr Weston's good wine', giving T. F. Powys the title for a book on a very different theme.

The daughter of a clergyman, and the sister of two more, Jane Austen had no difficulty in disposing of the awkward situation created by Emma's refusal of Mr Elton. Her heroine was spared the zig-zags of embarrassment unavoidable had she had to listen to Mr Elton's Christmas Day sermon. Foul weather kept her at home, though Mr Knightley braved snow and slush to be with the Christmas party, distressing Mr Woodhouse by the risk he was taking. John Knightley, whose ill-humour could cast a blight, was, on the other hand, delighted to be immured with his family. His prejudice against society does not seem to have been a handicap in his career in the law. Possibly he may have been feared as a bear dangerous to irritate.

Further embarrassment was spared Emma by the

departure of Mr Elton for Bath, in what could only be called a state of high dudgeon. Emma was then left to break down the illusion she had built up to Harriet, which she, Emma, had created single-handed. Miss Woodhouse had encouraged Harriet to regard her as an oracle, and the later had too lowly an opinion of herself to blame her benefactress, but talking Harriet out of love was more difficult than talking her into it. The sight of a trunk labelled the Revd Philip Elton, White-Hart, Bath, threw Harriet into a state of distress. Even some renewed contact with the Martins of Abbey Farm, the home she had spurned, failed to raise her spirits.

This glimpse of Mr Elton's trunk was the answer to one of the two questions set by Hope Mirrlees (which have been referred to in the Introduction). The questions were: 'What was Mr Elton's Christian name, and how do we know?' The answer being 'Philip', and it was seen by Harriet painted on his trunk.

And the second question: 'What was Mr Woodhouse's Christian name, and how do we know?' His name was 'Henry', and we know from his own lips, when Mr Woodhouse explained that his daughter Isabella had called her eldest son 'Henry'. He was proud of this filial devotion, which had, contrary to contemporary practice, given her husband's name 'John', only to her second-born son.

Contrary to fairy tale lore, the only two step-mothers in Jane Austen's major novels were entirely benign. Mrs Dashwood (*Sense and Sensibility*) was so delightful that her daughters' admirers were apt to be in love with her. Mrs Weston was only too anxious to welcome her husband's son, and prepared to love him, but for a while it did not seem that she would have the opportunity. Frank Churchill was expected, but once again wrote that he could not be spared from his attendance on Mrs Churchill, his adoptive mother.

Emma discussed this continual postponement with Mr Knightley. He, throughout a highly comic scene, displayed less than his usual liberality of mind. In face of teasing opposition from Emma, Mr Knightley insisted that Frank Churchill had no excuse for allowing himself to be kept from his natural father on the occasion of Mr Weston's remarriage. Emma rather overdid calculating the pleasure that the neighbourhood might enjoy when the long-delayed visit did take place. Emma had not learnt that few young men delight in hearing a pretty girl, in whom they have a property, postulate the charms of an unknown rival.

Her own peculiar interest in Frank Churchill as a possible husband for herself was, Emma believed shared by Mr and Mrs Weston. She did not, however, believe that any hint of such speculation had reached Mr Knightley. She could not understand the ill-humour with which Mr Knightley censured Frank Churchill for being known to have recently visited the fashionable resort of Weymouth, while neglecting to visit his father. Mr Knightley may not have understood why he should feel so irritated at Emma's expectation of pleasure from the visit of Mr Weston's son.

Paying a duty call on Miss Bates, and old Mrs Bates, was a social chore which Emma evaded unless her conscience was unusually active. The call, she knew, was only too likely to involve listening from the latest letter from Jane Fairfax, their niece and granddaughter. This orphan girl had been brought up by her late father's commanding officer, as a sister to his own daughter. Although he was powerless to bestow a dowry on Jane, he gave her every opportunity to gain the accomplishments that would enable her to be highly valued as a governess.

Emma could never bring herself to make a friend of Jane Fairfax. Mr Knightley accused her of jealousy of Miss Fairfax's superior talents, but Emma insisted that it was a reserve that she found impenetrable and repulsive. Although she had calculated that a letter from Jane Fairfax was not due and so might be escaped, Emma found that an unexpected letter had arrived. Jane Fairfax had written to say that medical advice urged her to seek her native air, as an aid to recovery from a malaise that had been plaguing her. Emma tried to do her best to make Jane welcome to Hartfield, but found Miss Fairfax's reserve as ever impenetrable.

One of Mr Knightley's complaints of Frank Churchill's neglect of his father had been that the excuse of being tied to the Churchills was specious. It was known at Highbury that he had been on his own, to Weymouth, and had there been slightly acquainted with Miss Fairfax. She had been on a visit there with the Campbells, but in reply to questions from Emma would only vouchsafe that she believed Frank Churchill to be generally considered a fine young man with pleasing manners.

Spas and watering places being notoriously perilous for bachelors, Highbury can hardly have been surprised to learn that, at Bath, Mr Elton had been hooked by a Miss Augusta Hawkins. Mr Elton's wounded pride had been quickly poulticed and, on his brief appearance before the wedding, Emma was startled to find how inferior she now thought him to be. The prospect of the arrival of Mr Elton's bride was, however, temporarily put aside, while High-bury had, at last, the pleasure of welcoming Mr Frank Churchill, whose long-delayed visit was finally so precipitate that he reached Randalls a good twelve hours before he was expected.

Emma was delighted to find him a lively and good-looking young man, obviously anxious to make a good impression on herself. Someone with more reflection and less imagination than Emma might have connected Frank's arrival with that of Jane Fair-fax, deducing that his insistence on calling on Miss Fairfax and her aunt at the earliest opportunity was more than a polite gesture. Emma smelt no rat, and had already built up one of her most preposterous theories. The Campbells' daughter had married a Mr Dixon, and her parents had gone to their son-in-law's estate in Ireland. To have left Jane behind seemed suspicious to Emma, and she developed an idea that there must have been a tendresse between Mr Dixon and Jane Fairfax, which would account for her exclusion from the Irish visit.

By his lively manner touched by gallantry, Frank Churchill managed to win Emma's confidence to the extent that she confided in him her suspicions about Jane Fairfax, and a too warm feeling between her and Mr Dixon. The delivery, from an unknown benefac-tor, of a piano-forte to the humble home of Jane's grandmother, increased the edifice of speculation building up by Emma and Frank. They agreed that the piano might well be a token of regard from Mr Dixon, and so sent anonymously.

These confidences between Emma and Frank had arisen at a dinner party in Highbury, which had ended in an impromptu dance. Frank Churchill then became eager that his parents should arrange a proper ball at Randalls. That dancing would give him an excuse for private conversation with Jane Fairfax was, of course, his motive, but he built up cover by claiming Emma as his preferred partner. Although Randalls was far from spacious, Frank Churchill insisted that by opening various doors the small rooms might become miraculously larger. These manoeuvres distressed Mr Woodhouse, who had a horror of draughts. There was even a dreadful moment when Mr Woodhouse threatened to consign Frank to the limbo of someone who was 'not quite the thing'. Immediately, Mrs Weston and Emma caused Frank to sit down, having shut the doors, but matters were hardly improved when Frank arrived at Hartfield with a new proposition.

Mr Churchill came to request the honour of Miss Woodhouse's hand for the first two dances for a ball to be given at the Crown Inn, Highbury, which possessed a ballroom now only used as a whist club. Mr Woodhouse was loath to accept this plan as an improvement. Terrible colds might result – inns were always damp – and he did not even know by sight the people who kept the Crown. He was further incensed by Frank's suggestion that the risk from cold would be so much less at the Crown than at Randalls. The only person likely to suffer would be Mr Perry the apothecary, who would have no patients for whom to prescribe.

To Mr Woodhouse, Mr Perry was both a valued consultant and an acquiescent friend, on to whom he could transfer many of his own fears of unhealthy influences. To suggest that Mr Perry should welcome patients as a source of income was, to Mr Woodhouse, an outrage. And why, he asked, should the Crown Inn be a safer venue for the ball than Randalls?

Frank explained that in a room built as a ballroom, there would be no need to open windows, and so run the risk of cold air on heated bodies. To Mr Woodhouse's horror at such an idea, Frank replied that he had known occasions when a thoughtless young person (himself might be suspected) had, surreptitiously, stepped behind a curtain and thrown, up a sash. 'Bless me! I could never have supposed it [said Mr Woodhouse]. But I live out of the world, and am often astonished at what I hear.' This could be called a summing-up of Mr Woodhouse's philosophy of life.

Mr Woodhouse was not alone in his disapproving attitude towards the prospective ball. Mr Knightley continued to show some illiberality of mind, professing that he would rather spend the evening going over his farm-steward's accounts. Only too soon he was able to do exactly that. With arrogance, verging on spiteful satisfaction in spoiling the enjoyment of others, Mrs Churchill declared herself to have become far too unwell to spare her adopted son. When Frank called to say goodbye to Emma, he was in a downcast mood. It almost seemed to Miss Woodhouse that he had it in mind to make a declaration of affection towards her, but, wishing to avoid a crisis, she steered the conversation away from such a danger.

Emma paid no attention to Frank's explanation that he had been obliged to spend some time waiting for Miss Bates to return home. He might be prepared to laugh at her ceaseless prattling on every subject, but he had no wish to be less than civil towards her by failing to bid her goodbye. Someone less inclined than Emma to build fantasy on intuition might have remarked that there must have been a far from short space when Frank Churchill would have been alone with Jane Fairfax, and only the drowsy Mrs Bates as chaperone.

After Frank's departure, Emma felt that his attentions had given her the right to be slightly, but deliciously, in love. In Frank's absence she could only, as it were, put a bookmarker in her feelings, and turn her attention to formally welcoming Mr Elton's bride. The etiquette of the period required that a call should be paid at the earliest moment, and when this had been returned the newly-wed couple should be entertained at a dinner party. After this threefold ritual, Emma's opinion of Mr Elton sank ever lower.

During her call at the vicarage, when she was accompanied by Harriet, she could find it possible to have some pity for Mr Elton. No man could be expected to enjoy being in the same room with the woman he had just married, the woman he had wanted to marry, and the woman he had been expected to marry. Mr Elton did not stand the test well, but it was when the call was returned that Emma found Mrs Elton to be both vulgar and pretentious. She put on airs as coming from a wider world, and patronised Miss Woodhouse for a shy provincial who needed to be brought on socially. Emma could not, however, ignore that civility required her to entertain the Eltons to dinner. Harriet was offered the invitation, but excused herself. Harriet felt uneasy at the idea of spending an evening with Mr Elton and what she still considered to be his charming wife.

Emma was now able, as she had always wished, to make a party of eight equal numbers by including Jane Fairfax, though this plan threatened to be upset by the advent of John Knightley. He was bringing his two eldest boys for a visit, and would find the dinner party an infliction. The elegant balance was, however, restored by the enforced absence of Mr Weston on business.

Mr Woodhouse's refusal to sit at the end of his own table was adamant, Mr Knightley in consequence acted as host. It can be assumed that the company sat down in the diagram seen below.

Mr George Knightley

Mrs Elton	Mrs Weston
Mr Woodhouse	Mr Elton
Miss Jane Fairfax	Miss Woodhouse

Mr John Knightley

Conversation before dinner had made it clear that Jane Fairfax, prone to catch cold though she was, had walked to the Highbury Post Office through a shower of rain. Jane refused to be convinced that she should only take her morning walk in fine weather. She was determined in rebuffing Mrs Weston's kind advice, and Mrs Elton's offer that 'one of our men, I forget his name' should collect the letters for the Bates household.

After dinner, Mrs Elton's officious patronage of Jane became increasingly presumptuous. She insisted that she would be perpetually on the watch for a situation of governess suitable to Jane's talents and accomplishments. No attention was paid to Jane's determination to take no steps until the Campbells had returned to Ireland. Jane's reference to registry offices in town where 'not quite human flesh but human intellect' was on sale, drew a shocked response from Mrs Elton. Jane, she thought, was having a fling at the slave trade. This had been abolished, as far as British ships were concerned, in 1807. Mrs Elton assured Jane that her rich brother-in-law, Mr Suckling, had been 'rather a friend of the abolition'.

Critics of Jane Austen's attitude towards public affairs have been known to say that when Sir Thomas Bertram was sent by the author to regulate his Antigua estate (*Mansfield Park*) or Captain Wentworth was instrumental in claiming the late Mr Smith's West Indies property for his widow, (*Persuasion*) she showed no awareness of the evils of slavery. It is true that Jane Austen did not mention slavery in this context. It is also true that the properties concerned were certainly worked by slave labour, but words put into the mouth of Jane Fairfax showed slavery to have been a matter on which Jane Austen had reflected, and found those who carried it on to be guilty of inhumanity.

'I did not mean, I was not thinking of the slave trade,' replied Jane, 'governess-trade, I assure you, was all that I had in view; widely different certainly as to the guilt of those who carry it on; but as to the greater misery of the victims, I do not know where it lies.' Miss Fairfax had the lowest possible opinion of the profession for which her kind protectors had taken such pains to qualify her. Mrs Elton was not one to apprehend the mildest joke, and continued to insist that she would pursue any hint of a desirable situation.

Mrs Elton's importunities were interrupted by the arrival of Mr Weston. Earlier, Emma, listening to the argument about fetching letters, had been struck by the unusual glow in Jane's complexion, as in someone cheered by a satisfactory errand. Emma's guess that Jane had collected a letter with good news was correct, but she assumed the letter was from the blameless Mr Dixon in Ireland. It never struck her that, when Mr Weston brought a letter from Frank saying that his adoptive parents were moving to London, Jane might have had earlier information, and so did not immediately respond to Mr Weston's wish for congratulations on Frank's prospective arrival.

Mrs Elton's patronage of Jane Fairfax grew ever more overwhelming, but her attitude to Emma rapidly chilled. Additionally, both the Eltons behaved in a contemptuous manner towards the unhappy Harriet, whose attachment to Mr Elton had obviously been what Jane Austen called an 'offering of conjugal unreserve'. With this evidence of the Eltons' unpleasant natures inescapably known to Jane Fairfax, Emma was astonished to learn that Jane, accustomed to good society, had been spending whole days with Mrs Elton. Mr Knightley, undiscouraged by the lack of respect Emma gave to his advice, pointed out that Mrs Elton paid attentions to Jane such as no one else, certainly not Emma, took the trouble to do.

Even the company of Mrs Elton, Mr Knightley pointed out, would be a relief from the ceaseless babble of Miss Bates' conversation. It might be tedious to hear Mrs Elton boasting of the wealth and importance of her sister Mrs Suckling of Maple Grove, but it would be at least a change from the running commentary of Miss Bates, whose every thought came forth in words: 'Well here we are at the passage. Two steps, Jane, take care of the two steps. Oh! No, there is but one. Well, I was persuaded there were two. How very odd! I was convinced there were two, and there is but one.'

This mild example of Miss Bates' chatter accompanied the supper procession of the ball that was finally held at the Crown Inn. The Churchills had left Enscombe with the hope of benefiting Mrs Churchill's health. They were now settled at Richmond, only nine miles from Highbury. Frank was immediately available, and the Westons arranged the ball with an appropriate supper. Before the supper interval, however, Emma had been outraged by a display of deliberate ill-manners from Mr Elton. The numbers, male and female, were equal. Consequently when Harriet Smith was sitting down, it was obvious that Mr Elton, clearly the spare man, was resolved not to ask her to dance. He resisted Mrs Weston, who as hostess pressed the matter, excusing himself as an old married man. Harriet was rescued from humiliation by Mr Knightley, not usually a dancer. Emma was delighted by his kindness, and by the fact that he had found Harriet more conversible than he had expected.

Undeterred by the disaster of her previous effort to find a husband for Harriet, Emma, deciding that she was not herself in love with Frank, thought his affections volatile, and began to think of a match between Mr Churchill and Miss Smith. The nebulous idea was already in her mind – 'happy the man who changes Emma for Harriet' – when a dramatic circumstance caused the idea to solidify. Frank Churchill happened to come upon Harriet when she was surrounded by a crowd of trampers or gypsies. He rescued her from their importunities, and escorted her back to Hartfield. This deliverance, it seemed to Emma, must make the most rational mind accept the inevitability of the couple becoming interested in each other. The idea was fertilised by Harriet's appeal to Emma to witness her destruction of two relics of Mr Elton which she had hoarded, the leadless stub of a pencil, and a piece of court plaster. These 'most precious treasures' had been hoarded in 'a pretty little Tunbridge-ware box', a touch which can only evoke one of the most charming lesser artefacts of Jane Austen's epoch.

Even more significant was Harriet's solemn declaration that she intended never to marry. She then admitted to being attached to a being far superior to herself, to whom, also, she owed a debt of gratitude. To Emma this could only mean Frank Churchill, rescuer of Harriet from the pack of gypsies. With the pride of the Churchills of Enscombe ever before her, Emma strove not to encourage hopes that would lead to another breaking of Harriet's heart. Rather pompously, she counselled her protégée to let 'his behaviour to be the guide of [Harriet's] sensations'. No name was mentioned between the young ladies, and it was agreed that silence should be preserved on the subject.

Mr Knightley had shown a disfavour to the personality of Frank Churchill, which had remained a mystery to Emma. She had not faced the idea that the Westons' almost open wish that Frank should pay court to herself would be clear to Mr Knightley. He had himself been challenged by Mrs Weston and Emma as to having a more than friendly interest in Jane Fairfax, but had denied it. Emma was strongly against any marriage which would be a threat to her nephew Henry's eventual inheritance of Donwell Abbey. With distrust of Frank's behaviour, Mr Knightley began to suspect that Frank's rather obvious gallantry towards Emma was cover for a double game with Jane Fairfax.

It was actually a game, a primitive ancestor of Scrabble, that confirmed Mr Knightley's suspicions. Frank had shewn himself acquainted with a piece of Highbury gossip that had not been passed on to him by Mrs Weston. When the game's letters were scattered across the table, Frank set a word to Miss Fairfax, which she worked on, and then pushed away with a faint smile. The word escaped mixing with the pack, and was pounced on by Harriet Smith. She proclaimed the word to be 'blunder', which caused Mr Knightley to feel that the impeccable Jane Fairfax might be called a 'deep one' to use a rather vulgar expression. After a giggly conference with Emma, Frank pushed another word towards Miss Fairfax. This turned out to be 'Dixon', and caused her obvious annoyance. She even refused to puzzle out what might have been an apology from Frank.

With this evidence of a secret understanding, Mr Knightley tackled Emma, who had after all been a partner to Jane's discomfiture. Emma tried, rather feebly, to laugh off the spelling game as a joke among the three parties concerned. She continued to suspect that Jane had had a tendresse for Mr Dixon, but she had become ashamed to have passed on the surmise to Frank. Mr Knightley felt obliged, for Emma's sake, to press the matter further. Had Emma any idea that there might be an attachment between Miss Fairfax and Mr Churchill? Emma, of course, laughed at the suggestion, assuring him that she knew it to be untrue, particularly on the side of Frank. She laughed even more at a match-making suggestion from Mr Knightley, and he went home in profound irritation.

No one was more aware than Jane Austen that, in a small social circle, it was the actual enemies who suffered most. Indeed their chief pain would be the tolerance from those for whom they had affection for neighbours they could not abide. This was the position between Emma and the Eltons. Her irritation came to a head over a project to visit Box Hill. Incidentally, for his edition of *Emma*, Doctor Chapman chose an illustration, late 18th or early 19th century, of the view from Box Hill, whose extent would reward any expedition.

To Miss Woodhouse the prospect of a pleasant day with her closest friends was wrecked by the incorrigible sociability of Mr Weston. More was always merrier to him, and he could not be prevented from including the Eltons in the Box Hill party. Mrs Elton's magnificent relations, the Sucklings, with their barouche landau, had postponed their visit, and Mr Weston, ignoring Emma's disapproval, argued that it would be churlish to exclude Mrs Elton. To add to Emma's sense of outrage, she realised that, as a young unmarried girl, she might be said to be under the chaperonage of the Vicar's odious wife.

A lame carriage-horse jeopardised the scheme, and Mrs Elton was so disconsolate that Mr Knightley invited her to come and make a feast of the strawberries at Donwell. This invitation was given when Mr Knightley was calling on Mrs Elton, presumably, as etiquette required, after the dinner-party at which he had begun to suspect an understanding between Jane Fairfax and Frank Churchill.

Mrs Elton was enchanted at the distinction she felt to be conferred on her by this invitation. Mr Knightley, however, parried her attempts to invite his neighbours. Only one lady, he said, would have *carte blanche* to issue invitations to Donwell, and until this lady, Mrs Knightley, was in existence he would do the inviting himself. This speech to Mrs Elton was the first indication that Mr Knightley was not prepared to spend his life as the leading bachelor landowner of the neighbourhood, a benevolent neuter, with his brother John's son Henry as his heir.

If Mrs Elton considered the strawberry party to be a particular compliment to herself, the other guests made equal assumptions. It was even found possible to persuade Mr Woodhouse that courtesy to his elder daughter's brother-in-law required him to make the expedition to Donwell. This was part of Mr Knightley's hospitable plan, but he could have dispensed with Mr Weston's promise to summon Frank from Richmond for the occasion. Emma had now assigned Frank to her protégée, Harriet, but awkward events at Donwell, and at the Box Hill picnic shook her out of her complacency.

At Donwell the novel might be said to take a more sombre turn, though the day started well. Emma found everything to approve in the men and estate to which her sister Isabella had connected the Woodhouses. Jane Austen made no attempt to present Donwell as a romantic feast for the imagination, as she was later to describe Northanger Abbey. Donwell had some handsome rooms, but rambled in a comfortable way, 'the residence of a family of such true gentility, untainted in blood and understanding'.

Once the party arrived at the strawberry beds, Mrs Elton excelled herself in a prolixity of nonsense, but when the party was resting in the shade, Emma was distressed to hear a direct attack on Jane Fairfax. A governess was needed in a family called Smallridge, living only four miles from the glories of Mrs Suckling's mansion, Maple Grove. Refusing to hear Jane's protests, Mrs Elton was determined to bully the recalcitrant girl, for her own good, into accepting Mrs Smallridge's situation.

It was at this point in the novel that clouds began to darken the normally clear sky of Emma's existence. She watched without apprehension Mr Knightley talking to Harriet Smith with unusual particularity, while they gazed at the view of Manor Farm. (Jane Austen was teased by her family for describing Manor Farm as lying in an 'orchard in blossom', a natural impossibility at midsummer in strawberry time.) Watching this *tête-à-tête*, Emma was pleased that Mr Knightley no longer dismissed Harriet as what a later age might have labelled 'the original dumb blonde'.

It had been Jane Fairfax's smooth reserve which had originally repelled Emma, but on the afternoon of the party at Donwell they came closer to intimacy than ever before. Emma met Jane, who was insisting on walking home by herself. She brushed aside Emma's protests and offers of an escort or a carriage. Jane's exclamation at the comfort of being sometimes alone moved Emma to compassion. It was painful to think of the delicate girl, with all her talents, passing her days in confined space under the ceaseless barrage of her devoted aunt's conversation.

Mr Knightley had laid out collections of cameos and prints to entertain Mr Woodhouse, who, having plodded through the display, wanted to repeat the process with Emma. They had, however, only arrived at what Jane Austen charmingly called St Mark's Place, Venice, when Frank Churchill, nearly despaired of as having been once again the victim of Mrs Churchill's sick whims, walked into the room. With a churlishness remote from his usual good manners, he complained of the heat, and his own lateness.

Frank said that he had already met one of the party walking home, absolute madness in this weather, he added.

Anyone less set than Emma in her own opinions about relationships among her friends, would not have found it difficult to suspect that Frank's meeting with Jane Fairfax was the cause of his extreme ill-humour. He did not bring himself to mention her name, but his symptoms were those of a lover deprived of a meeting with the one he loved. Emma, herself, rejoiced at being no longer in love with someone so much at the mercy of the weather, but thought that this was a failing that Harriet's sweet nature would easily support.

Mr Woodhouse's display of the treasures of Donwell to his daughter had reached as far as views of Swisserland, the spelling used by Jane Austen, when Frank returned slightly revived by cold meat and spruce beer. He still appeared restless, in a general way, and announced himself as determined to see Swisserland in reality. He even persuaded himself that Mrs Churchill might be ordered abroad for her health. Rebuked by Emma for complaining that he was sick of his situation, being a prisoner of luxury with out aim or occupation, he could only insist that he lived a life of frustration. Frank did, however, agree to join the party to Box Hill on the following day, if Emma wanted him as a fellow-guest.

Indisputably, the party to Box Hill was haunted by the Little God Pan, who, according to E. M. Forster, disrupts unsuccessful picnics. Doctor Chapman appeared to have an open mind as to whether Highbury was, in fact, Cobham, which is the same distance from Box Hill, seven miles, as Highbury was stated to be. From wherever they started, two carriages were filled by five ladies and Mr Elton, while the other three gentlemen rode on horseback. When they reached Box Hill, a cliff jutting out from the North Downs, there was general admiration for a splendid view, eventually fading into the blue mists of the Thames Valley. After this moment of harmony, however, the party broke up into groups that did not coalesce.

In the racing stable of Jane Austen's cads, Frank Churchill could not be called a front runner. He lacked the recklessness which led Willoughby (*Sense and Sensibility*) down the path of the seducer, the scoundrelly charm of Wickham (*Pride and Prejudice*) or the cold-blooded calculation which made Mr Elliot (*Persuasion*) agreeable in society, but ruthless in personal relationships. At Box Hill, however, Frank behaved in a manner which embarrassed the company, with the exception of Emma, to whom his attentions passed the boundary of common civility into flirtatious particularity.

Having decided that Frank was genuinely in love with her but that her feelings for him, such as they had been, had faded, Emma, as had been seen, had allocated him to Harriet. This did not, however, prevent her from responding to Frank's provocative conversation. Very few women would object to an admirer showing a touch of auld lang syne, but Mr Churchill's attentions were more positive. He was prepared to declare in accents to be heard at 'Mickleham on one side, and Dorking on the other' that he had first seen Miss Woodhouse in February. The rest of the company looked on in varying degrees of dumb disapproval.

Matters came to a head with a declaration from Frank. 'Ladies and gentlemen, I am ordered by Miss

Woodhouse (who, wherever she is presides) to say that she desires to know what you are all thinking of' . . . Mrs Elton swelled at the idea of Miss Woodhouse's presiding; Mr Knightley's answer was the most distinct. 'Is Miss Woodhouse sure she would like to hear what we are all thinking of?'

If formality, a sharp weapon in Jane Austen's armoury, was abandoned, and 'Emma' 'Augusta' and 'George' substituted for 'Miss', 'Mrs', and 'Mr', the paragraph would lose some of its force. Mr Knightley's comment on the other hand, is an example of the timelessness of Jane Austen's style, and would not be out of place in any contemporary dialogue.

Emma now disgraced herself by a mock deferential remark to Miss Bates. Frank Churchill had requested the company, as Emma's mouthpiece, to contribute one very clever thing, two moderately clever things, or three things very dull indeed. Humbleminded and cheerful about her own failings, Miss Bates had declared she would be certain to say three very dull things every time she opened her mouth. Emma's manner, in which she assured Miss Bates that only *three* things were necessary, was so serious that it took a moment for the victim to detect the mockery. If Miss Bates was distressed that Emma thought her a voluble bore, Mr Knightley was outraged at this heartless teasing of someone growing old in poverty, and likely to grow poorer.

This act of unkindness, however, paled before Frank Churchill's behaviour vis-à-vis Jane Fairfax, even though the onlookers were not aware of the undercurrents. Having derided the Eltons, who, in fairness, did appear reasonably congenial, for marrying on an acquaintance made in public, Jane was goaded into declaring that such a hasty attachment might lead to unhappiness, but to a firm mind recovery should be possible. Accepting this dictum, Frank then proceeded to commission Emma to find him a wife. Assuming that he would spend two years abroad, he would then come to Miss Woodhouse for a wife, only stipulating that she would be very lively and have hazel eyes. Still fixed on the idea of matching Frank with Harriet, Emma accepted the commission. In two years, she thought, Harriet might well be educated into liveliness, though not even Emma could expect to change the colour of Harriet's eyes.

After this demonstration of irresponsibility about his future by Frank Churchill, not surprisingly Jane suggested to her aunt that they should join Mrs Elton. Miss Bates immediately misidentified the Vicar's wife, only to find it was one of the ladies in the Irish-car party. This would presumably have been an 'outside car' (as opposed to an 'inside car' with its sheltering curtains), sometimes known, not to the Irish, as a 'jaunting car'. It would be interesting to know if such carriages were sufficiently common in Surrey for Miss Bates to recognise one on sight.

Mr Knightley's rebuke for Emma's unkindness to Miss Bates made her determined to make amends by increased attentions to the Bates and to Jane. Ever precipitate in action, Emma called on the family on the morning after the picnic. She found Jane was prostrated by headache and could not receive the caller. It was thus that it fell to Miss Bates to explain that Jane had, suddenly, the previous evening, decided to accept the situation as governess to Mrs Smallridge, promoted by Mrs Elton and previously refused by Jane. Her decision to accept the situation had been taken after chance had informed her that

Frank had returned to Richmond. Emma failed to notice this clue as a pointer to the couple's behaviour.

Efforts to make up for past neglect met with continual rebuffs from Miss Fairfax, who declared herself too indisposed for a drive in the Woodhouse carriage, although she was reported as having been seen wandering in the fields nearby. The one person who could see nothing wrong in Jane going out as a governess was Mr Woodhouse. He saw her as a second Miss Taylor (Mrs Weston) in the house of Mrs Elton's friends, only hoping she would not grieve them by marrying.

Suddenly, speculations on Jane's future were blotted out by one of the most satisfactory pieces of news in the history of the novel. The great Mrs Churchill was dead. Her husband was thought to be displaying a respectable amount of grief for a wife whose continual profession of ill-health had been finally vindicated. Emma thought that Harriet was behaving with laudable composure, considering that the main obstacle to her possible marriage to Frank Churchill had been removed. It was well known that Mr Churchill was putty in the hands of Frank, as was shortly to be proved in highly dramatic fashion.

As has been pointed out earlier, Jane Austen abstained from revealing if there was issue from the marriages of her heroines. In her own family and immediate neighbourhood, maternal mortality was high, and this may have affected her approach to the subject of childbirth. When her brother James' second wife was expecting her first child, there were two deaths in childbed in the neighbourhood. The family, rightly, refrained from mentioning this depressing news to Mrs James Austen, who, luckily, gave birth without disaster.

Mrs Weston, presumably in her thirties, was however allowed to conceive. Her pregnancy caused her
to be absent from the Box Hill party, where she
might have been an emollient influence. It was
anxiety for her safety that caused apprehension to
Emma when, about ten days after Mrs Churchill's
death, Mr Weston arrived at Hartfield to ask if Emma
would immediately accompany him to Randalls. He
reassured Emma about his wife, but insisted that
Mrs Weston alone could 'break the news' to Miss
Woodhouse. Mr Knightley had recently gone to visit
his brother's family in Brunswick Square. Emma had
parted from him in more of an emotional turmoil
than she herself realised. At the idea that the bad
news might concern one of the Knightleys, Emma's
agitation was such that it needed a solemn denial
from Mr Weston to calm her. The relief set her
imagination off on one last fling. Could Mr Churchill
of Enscombe have been leading a double life, and
now revealed a family of illegitimate children,
thereby disinheriting Frank?

The bombshell that actually awaited Emma was
less catastrophic, if almost equally startling. With a
fear that she might be delivering a blow to the heart
of her dear Emma, Mrs Weston revealed that Frank
Churchill and Jane Fairfax had been secretly, but
positively, engaged, even before Frank had first come
to Randalls. Although able to assure Mrs Weston that
she felt no pang at the news, Emma was appalled. She
had allowed Frank to assist her in her fantasy that
love was simmering between Jane and Mr Dixon,
but far worse was the knowledge that she had once
again encouraged Harriet to attach herself where no
return was possible.

Although she could not entirely conceal her feelings that Frank had unfairly tricked her into an humiliating position, while laughing at her behind her back with Jane, Emma was not petty-minded. Having convinced Mrs Weston that any fancy she had felt for Frank had been evanescent, she was able to congratulate Mr Weston. He was always inclined to take a cheerful view, and gladly accepted Emma's assurance that he would be the lucky possessor of an exceptionally beautiful and accomplished daughter-in-law. Mrs Churchill, barely deposited in the family vault, might be thought to be turning over at this reversal of her tyranny, but, as Mrs Weston remarked, 'What a blessing it is, when undue influence does not survive the grave!'

Distressed though Emma was at the prospect of breaking the news of the engagement to Harriet, her feelings were as nothing to those from which she suffered when the interview had taken place. She had promised secrecy to the Westons, but felt she must exempt Harriet from the promise. Emma might have known that no secret would long be safe with Mr Weston. Harriet came bustling to Hartfield all agog with 'the oddest news that ever was'. She had met Mr Weston, and learnt what had so rapidly ceased to be a secret. Harriet's carefree curiosity startled Emma, and she found herself obliged to assure Harriet that, had she had any idea of the engagement, she would have warned Harriet against having hopes of Frank Churchill.

Harriet was equally taken aback by Emma's assumption that she loved Frank. After a minute or two, in which Emma's apprehension became terror, it transpired that when Emma was concentrating on Mr Churchill, Harriet's sights were set on Mr Knightley. Certain that Frank's rescue of Harriet from the gypsies had been mentioned when she had given Harriet some not discouraging advice, Emma insisted that it was Frank that they had discussed. It was here that Harriet made a rare attempt to stand up to her patroness. With good reason, she exclaimed, 'Oh! Miss Woodhouse, how you do forget!'

Forgetful or not, this was for Miss Woodhouse the most unexpected and shattering climax of her attempts to educate Harriet, mentally or socially. Down the years Emma had been accustomed to take for granted that she was the prime object of Mr Knightley's interest. The sudden realisation that she had, unawares, encouraged a rival was a soul-searing moment. With the shock, came the revelation that Mr Knightley must marry no one but herself, though words quoted back to her by Harriet conveyed a terrible feeling that Harriet might not be unreasonable to think that Mr Knightley was becoming attached to her.

The foundation for this assumption had been laid when Harriet, brutally humiliated by Mr Elton, had been rescued and led out to dance by Mr Knightley. With an effort of self-control, Emma managed to conceal the shock given by the once humble Miss Smith's confidence that the match would not be impossible. Harriet was dismissed with as much encouragement as Emma could give to a snake in the grass, fostered by herself. When alone, Emma's feelings broke out in an anguished cry, 'Oh God! That I had never seen her!'

As if on cue, the summer weather fled, leaving Emma indoors to the gloom of her own thoughts and the view of a garden battered by wind and rain. Few things are more depressing than a wet summer evening that lingers on implacably, but by the following afternoon the sun was shining on a garden sweet scented after the storm. The habit of being fortunate was ingrained in Emma's character, and she was never totally cast down for long. When Mr Perry arrived with an hour to spare for Mr Woodhouse, Emma escaped into the garden.

Once out of doors, her spirits had begun to rise, even from the contemplation of the tangled web she had woven, by practising deceit on herself. She had imagined Mr Knightley to be still in London, and so was surprised to find him joining her in the garden, but it was hardly a surprise that he had heard of the engagement of Frank and Jane from Mr Weston. When Emma realised that Mr Knightley had come into the garden to see if she was suffering the pangs of rejection, Emma explained that her heart was untouched. As she pointed out, she felt as much embarrassment in denying that she was in love with Frank as she would have had in admitting it.

Mr Knightley now put his fate to the touch and won it all, the all being Emma's heart. He could not, of course, know that it was Harriet's claim to be attaching him to herself which had startled Emma into the apprehension of losing him. In fact, unless he had actually eloped with Harriet, Mr Knightley would have had no chance of not marrying Emma, once she had made up her mind that she could not tolerate anyone except herself as the châtelaine of Donwell Abbey.

Mr Knightley's proposal and Emma's acceptance brought everything out into the sunlight. Not even the necessity of yet again breaking it to Harriet that she was the one preferred nor the thought of dis-inheriting her little nephew Henry caused Emma to hesitate. Mr Knightley, always subconsciously jealous of Frank Churchill as a possible suitor for Emma, now found that his fears were unfounded, and he was even prepared to admit that Frank might have some redeeming points.

Among Jane Austen's most engaging character-istics was the ability to take a sly dig at her characters when pomposity threatened to become heavy. Mr Knightley had always held up Jane Fairfax to Emma as an example of a cultivated woman, Emma lacking the application necessary to become Jane's equal. But even when praising Jane's accomplishments Mr Knightley had qualified his admiration by condemn-ing the want of openness in her character. Jane's secret engagement now explained this reserve, but Mr Knightley still inveighed against finesse and mystery as perverting the understanding.

He put this point to the promised Mrs Knightley, 'My Emma, does not everything prove more and more the beauty of truth and sincerity in all our dealings with each other?' Emma found agreement to be politic, making a mental exception for her dealings with Harriet. She buried this lapse from truth and sincerity in the graveyard allotted to truths better, for the moment, left untold. Emma felt she might, in the future, reveal the story of Harriet's attachment, but it might be hoped that wiser counsels prevailed. Mr Knightley was hardly a man who would relish having been the centre of a mistaken passion.

Harriet did, indeed, show some resentment when Emma informed her of her engagement, and to get Harriet out of the way became a vital first step in reducing an intimacy plunged in embarrassment. Isa-bella Knightley was always the friend of ill-health, and as Harriet needed to consult a dentist, she was dispatched to Brunswick Square. It was now that Mr

Knightley showed how superior was his talent for making matches to that of Miss Woodhouse.

After Harriet had been absent or some days, Mr Knightley came to see her with news that staggered, but delighted Emma. Robert Martin had been asked to take some business papers to John Knightley, who relaxed his social distaste sufficiently to ask Mr Martin to join a family party to Astley's Circus. With even more complicity, John Knightley went so far as to ask Robert Martin to dinner, and this time his proposal to Harriet was accepted. Emma's relief was increased by recalling that, only a short time before, Harriet had been incensed at the idea that she might even be suspected of caring for Robert Martin. The relief was all the greater because, though Emma had not doubted that Harriet would find a replacement for Mr Knightley, it was difficult to believe that even Harriet could be in love with more than three men in a single year.

Mrs Weston, now the mother of her own daughter, was particularly pleased with Mr Knightley's self-sacrifice in being prepared to settle at Hartfield with Emma. This solved the problem of caring for Mr Woodhouse. Frank Churchill and Jane Fairfax had now the prospect of their own elegant home at Enscombe, but when the Westons had hoped to make a match between Frank and Emma, Mr Woodhouse had always been a stumbling block to their schemes. The thought of Frank, high-spirited and free spoken, in daily clash with Mr Woodhouse's delicate ways, was not an idea to be regarded with equanimity.

The Eltons, the only disagreeable characters in the novel, took the news of Emma's engagement with a very bad grace. Mrs Elton, regarding all men as potential slaves, considered Mr Knightley's escape into matrimony as an insult to herself. The Reverend Philip Elton was now required to marry two couples. The first bride, Harriet Smith, he had spurned on account of her unknown origin. Her male parent turned out to be below gentility, but able to bestow a handsome dowry on this bye-blow. The second bride, Emma Woodhouse, had, in her turn, spurned Mr Elton. This was a wedding that Mrs Elton did not attend, but she sneered at the lack of finery when listening to her husband's account of the ceremony.

The paths of Emma and Harriet inevitably separated, their friendship sinking into amiable neighbourliness. When they did meet, it can be speculated that the year in which they had voyaged together over a sea of passion, in a storm-tossed boat, must have been increasingly recollected as an improbable dream.

5

Northanger Abbey

THE HISTORY OF A HEROINE

Among the young ladies who played the leads in Jane Austen's major novels, Catherine Morland may not have been the brightest intellectually, but she was, in many ways, the most endearing. Catherine's early life reflected some of her creator's own upbringing, in a vicarage crowded with children. Before she qualified as a heroine, Catherine was a romp, who loved to roll down the green slope behind her home, as Jane Austen herself might well have delighted to do. The little hoyden, however, grew up to be a girl of promising looks, and so became fit to be launched on her romantic career.

When Jane Austen was suddenly faced with the news that her father had decided to retire from the living of Steventon, her birthplace, and to settle in Bath, her reaction was spectacular. She fainted away on the spot. Her view of Bath was that of Anne Elliot in *Persuasion*. She did not like the city of Aquae Sulis, and did not believe that it agreed with her. But as an author she was prepared to take a balanced attitude, and to send the delighted Catherine Morland there with every promise of enjoyment.

Although Jane Austen pointed out that it was a handicap for the Squire of a heroine's parish to have no son, Mr Allen, the chief landed proprietor of Fullerton, where the Reverend Richard Morland held the living, did his best to remedy this failure. He invited Catherine to join him and his wife on a visit to Bath.

The focus of *Northanger Abbey*, it would be fair to say, was the ragging of the type of romance that might be called Gothic, of which Mrs Radcliffe, author of the *Mysteries of Udolpho* and many others in the same vein, was perhaps the most famous exponent. Jane Austen combined a highly scientific pulling of Mrs Radcliffe's leg with a powerful analysis of the shame felt by those detected in reading a novel. It may be permissible, at this point to quote the novelist Richard Hughes' remark, 'The archetypal non-reader of fiction was Hitler'.

In defence of the novel, a branch of literature whose practitioners have been described by Margaret Kennedy, dedicated novelist, as Outlaws on Parnassus, Jane Austen let fly.

'Although our productions have afforded more extensive and unaffected pleasure than those of any other literary corporation in the world, no species of composition has been so much decried,' Jane Austen wrote, with a white hot pen. She went on to describe the novel as a literary form despised by many, but 'in short, only some work in which the greatest powers of the mind are displayed, in which the most thorough knowledge of human nature, the happiest delineation of its varieties, the liveliest effusions of wit and humour are conveyed to the world in the best-chosen language.' Few, even among non-novel readers, would dispute that this might be a perfect summary of the virtues of Jane Austen's own work.

Unsuitability of spouses to each other was a recurrent theme in Jane Austen's novels. Mr and Mrs Allen, the patrons of Catherine Morland, were, as a couple, a mild example of this mismatch, he being an intelligent sensible man, she a masterpiece of mental vacuity. Mrs Allen might have had no beauty, wit or accomplishment, but she had a passion for dress and fashion, with an accompanying desire for social events. No heroine could have wished for a more complaisant chaperone.

The first few days at Bath were a disappointment, no acquaintances, no partners for Catherine. An introduction at the Lower Rooms, however, improved matters. The master of ceremonies, a position subsequently filled by a great-great uncle of Cyril Connolly, introduced a young clergyman to Miss Morland. The Reverend Henry Tilney was distinctly taken by Catherine's simplicity, which approached literal-mindedness, and although he disappeared after their first meeting, she had hopes to see him again.

Mrs Allen's steady complaint of no acquaintances in Bath was relieved by the chance meeting with a friend from her schooldays. Mrs Thorpe had the advantage of a family of six children, but Mrs Allen's keen eye immediately appraised the lace on Mrs Thorpe's pelisse as being not half so handsome as that which decorated her own. The three Miss Thorpes were then presented to Catherine, and her education in the stratagems of young ladies with roving eyes began.

Catherine was surprised at the Thorpe family's

familiarity with her brother James, until she remembered that James had stayed with an Oxford friend
of the name of Thorpe. The eldest Miss Thorpe,
Isabella, a beauty, at once made a set at Miss Morland, not entirely from personal predilection. To
anyone with more experience of the paths of flirtation, it would soon have become plain that Isabella
Thorpe had designs on James Morland, but Catherine
was too naive even to tease her new friend on the
subject.

When the weather was bad, Isabella Thorpe and
Catherine Morland shut themselves up to read novels
with a dedication worthy of Madame Bovary. On
fine days, the pair haunted the Pump Room, where
Catherine's innocence of the technique of denigrating
any young man who might be a promising quarry,
might have been tedious to Isabella, had the latter
not had a strong reason to ingratiate herself with
Catherine. When Isabella complained of the offensive
stares of two young men, and Catherine suggested a
means of avoiding them, Isabella ignored her friend's
simplicity, and set off in hot pursuit. The chase was
halted only by the sudden appearance of a gig, driven
by Isabella's brother, John Thorpe, with Catherine's
brother, James, as his passenger.

Catherine, delighted to see her brother, artlessly
imagined that he had come to Bath out of brotherly
affection. She had totally failed to understand Isabella's
hints about Mr Morland. Isabella's brother was a
bewilderment to Catherine. John Thorpe's pose as a
good-hearted rattle concealed a high level of fantasy,
and a disregard for truth, touched with malice. His
mother had praised her eldest as clever and popular
when talking to Mrs Allen. His greeting hardly bore
out the description. 'Ah, mother! How do you

do? . . . Where did you get that quiz of a hat, it makes you look like an old witch?'

In the meantime Henry Tilney had returned to Bath, bringing with him his sister Eleanor, and their formidable father, General Tilney. Torn between the elegant Tilneys and the more vulgar Thorpes, Catherine found herself walking a social tight-rope. Although his children's spirits were unaccountably depressed in his presence, the General was most affable to this new friend of his son and daughter.

It was impossible for Catherine to realise that John Thorpe, fancying Catherine, had deceived himself into believing that she was the heiress of Mr Allen. Pleased to be seen talking to such a distinguished man, John Thorpe had passed on this surmise as a fact to General Tilney. The latter immediately decided that Catherine would be a well-dowered bride for his son, Henry. That John Thorpe obviously wished to claim Catherine for himself, caused the General not the smallest hesitation. Morally speaking, the owner of Northanger Abbey and the rattling undergraduate were on the same level.

The next widening of Catherine's experience came with the engagement of her brother James to the dazzling Isabella. The Reverend Richard Morland, when applied to for his consent and support, behaved as handsomely as the father of ten children could be expected to behave. There would, necessarily, be a wait of two or three years until James was old enough to take the living that his father was to resign to him. Then it was that the strain of calculation in Isabella's character became apparent. To be engaged for even two years, and then to marry on an income of £400 was not a prospect that she relished. Catherine excited by the engagement of her brother and her bosom friend, still could feel that matters were not quite right, but was able to make excuses for Isabella.

Discomfort increased when Captain Frederick Tilney arrived to join his family. Thinking a great deal of himself, this young man refused the suggestion of dancing at a public ball, until he saw Miss Thorpe sitting down. James had left to tell his father of their engagement, and Isabella had declared that she would not dance in the absence of her fiancé. Catherine, typically, took Isabella's word to represent a fixed purpose, and was distinctly surprised when she found that her friend and Captain Tilney had joined the set in which she was partnered by Henry.

From then on the Morlands, brother and sister were made increasingly uncomfortable by Frederick Tilney's attentions to Isabella. Catherine, herself, was, however, diverted by an invitation to visit Northanger Abbey. The invitation came, as etiquette required, from Eleanor, but was obviously the work of the General. He was determined to whisk away this, as he supposed, little heiress from the fortune-hunters of Bath. Catherine was only aware of the romance of being invited to a real abbey, with no conception of her host's calculations. She bought a new straw bonnet, and wore it for the journey.

Allowing for his self-deception, the General may have behaved prudently, John Thorpe having pressed his suit by a letter to his sister. Catherine was astounded, and denied all encouragement, softening her refusal by telling Isabella that they would still be sisters. The latter said, thoughtfully, that there were more ways than one of bringing this about. She had, by now, cast a fly over Frederick Tilney, but until she had this fine fat fish on her line, Isabella was not prepared to throw back the tiddler, James Morland.

Invited to breakfast before starting for Northanger Catherine was overwhelmed by the affability of General Tilney. This included a lecture to his son Frederick on his disrespect to Miss Morland in coming late to breakfast. The Captain accepted the dressing-down in silence, but was heard to whisper to his sister that he would be thankful when the family had departed. This was not accomplished without a further display of temper by the General, and Catherine had difficulty in rescuing her new writing-case from being thrown out of the carriage.

For the last part of the journey of thirty miles to Northanger, the General decreed that Henry should drive Catherine in his curricle. This was after a tedious wait to bait the horses at Petty France, which would lead one to suppose that Northanger lay somewhere north east of Cirencester. Infinitely amused by Catherine's idea of the sinister potentialities of Northanger Abbey, Henry sketched in the sort of welcome the young lady had the right to expect. This included a bedroom of sombre aspect, far from earshot of the rest of the household. After two or three nights, Henry suggested, a storm blowing through the tapestry would indicate the entrance to a sequence of secret chambers.

Having mentioned drops of blood, a dagger and the remains of an instrument of torture, Henry allowed the fiction that Catherine would unlock a gold and ebony cupboard, where she would find a roll of paper containing the story of 'the unhappy Matilda'. At this point Henry's imagination and his gravity gave out completely.

He could only beg Catherine to use her own

imagination. Deliciously thrilled by Henry's suggestion of the Gothic horror awaiting her, Catherine was
disappointed to find herself arrived at a handsome
gentleman's seat, with only a few pointed windows
to link it with a monastic past. Familiarity with
Stoneleigh Abbey, the seat of her mother's family
the Leighs, allowed Jane Austen to visualise the disappointment that a student of Mrs Radcliffe's novels
would feel at fresh and modern surroundings, when
cobwebs and sinister mustiness had been hoped for.

Determined to have a mystery to explore, Catherine concentrated on General Tilney. Although his
flattering attentions to herself continued, she came
to the conclusion that his sometimes uneasy temper
might be interpreted as springing from a mind tor-
tured by remorse. Catherine went so far as to suspect
her host of having murdered his wife, or possibly of
having sequestered her in a wing of the Abbey. He
would be keeping her alive with a supply of coarse
food, given to her at night by stealth.

A previous discovery in her bedroom of what she
hoped to be a manuscript of some tragic tale turned
out to be the bills of a washerwoman and a farrier,
but Catherine, seeking a bloody trail, was undaunted.
With some cunning she arranged to make a foray,
on her own into what she believed to be the ancient
part of the Abbey. It would be here that Mrs Tilney
might well be imprisoned. She had miscalculated.
The bedroom of the supposedly late Mrs Tilney was,
in fact, in the most recently built wing, and was
palpably untenanted. While she was digesting the
collapse of her gruesome theory, there was a clatter
of footsteps up the stairs, and Henry Tilney, as surprised as herself, stood before her.

Catherine, truthfully, said that she had been to see

Mrs Tilney's bedroom, in which, presumably, she had died. Pressed by Henry, she admitted that she suspected a mystery about the death, as she understood all Mrs Tilney's children had been absent. Henry could only assure her that he and Frederick had been constantly at their mother's bedside. (She had, apparently, died from a recurrent gastro-enteritis) More or less guessing at the lurid suspicions of Catherine's imagination, he pointed out that, in their century of Christian enlightenment, the disappearance of the châtelaine of Northanger could not have gone unremarked in the neighbourhood. Henry begged 'dearest Miss Morland' to consider what terrible ideas she had been nursing, and his tenderness must have dried Catherine's tears of repentance.

Catherine's suspicions of General Tilney as a murderer may have been more comprehensible to Henry than filial prudence allowed him to admit. She was to learn only too soon that her host's words reflected neither his real opinions, nor his actions. She had settled down to enjoy her visit with only the wonder that she had had no word from Isabella, when a letter from her brother James upset her composure at the breakfast table.

Fortunately, General Tilney was absorbed in his newspaper and his cocoa (hardly a General's choice for breakfast in later years) and did not notice Catherine's distress at her letter. The poor girl fled to her bedroom, and, as was inevitable in the days of plentiful domestic staff, found housemaids in possession. Henry and Eleanor, kindly, left her to cry in the drawing-room, and only when she had recovered enough to return to the breakfast-room, did they learn why her brother's letter had thrown her into such distress.

There were few emotions particular to young girls that Jane Austen had not fathomed. She knew that the first engagement to marry in a young girl's circle has the unique freshness of novelty. James Morland's letter to his sister shattered Catherine's dream of the marriage of her brother and her bosom friend, the first friend she had made outside her family. James wrote that not only had he parted from Isabella Thorpe, but he expected that her engagement to Captain Frederick Tilney would be announced very shortly. James concluded with a warning to Catherine to be careful how she should give her heart.

Henry and Eleanor were not only astonished at their brother committing himself to a penniless beauty, but also at his risking the certain anger of their father. Catherine's quotation of their father's liberal sentiments on the subject of money being merely a means to secure his children's happiness caused only embarrassment to those children. Perhaps trying to bring a more cheerful thought to Catherine, Henry suggested that the only hope of Frederick escaping the predatory Isabella would be the sight of better prey, such as a baronet. He even proposed to fetch a newspaper and inspect the new arrivals at Bath.

Expecting that Frederick would arrive at Northanger to announce his engagement, Catherine was assured by Henry and Eleanor that nothing was more improbable. There was no need for her to return home precipitately, as she had begged to do. The comfort of her friends' sympathy even led her to agree that Isabella's unscrupulous behaviour had not destroyed all her enjoyment of life.

Catherine was, however, struck by Henry and Eleanor's certainty that Frederick's engagement would be badly received by their father. Henry firmly refused to soften the blow by any hint, saying that Frederick had certainly better tell his own story, half of which would be more than enough from the General's point of view. The General himself continued to behave with partiality towards Catherine. He added to his attentions by proposing that he, his daughter and their guest should drive the twenty miles to Woodston, and 'eat their mutton' with Henry, vicar of that parish.

Still unable to believe that the General's words were at odds with his real opinions, Catherine was downcast to find that Henry had to leave Northanger two days before the excursion to Woodston, in order as he put it to 'frighten his old housekeeper out of her wits'. To Catherine's reminder that his father had asked for no special effort to be made, Henry could only wish, for his father's sake and his own, that Miss Morland might be right.

It was at Woodston that General Tilney's proxy courtship of Catherine rose to new heights. Having decided that she, supposed heiress of Mr Allen, was a desirable wife for Henry, a detached onlooker might well have thought that he fancied the idea of a pretty daughter-in-law, settled conveniently for the pursuit of a paternal flirtation. His desire to please even overcame disgust at the melted butter being oiled, and there being no cold meat on the sideboard. After drawing a satisfactory amount of praise for the sitting-room, still unfurnished, that would obviously belong to Henry's wife, the General failed to get Catherine's opinions about carpets and curtains. She felt, not unreasonably, sure that the General would welcome her as a daughter, but was uncertain if his son would ask her to be his wife. As things turned out Catherine was wrong on both points.

At last a letter arrived from Isabella Thorpe, a letter which Jane Austen must have enjoyed composing. With many apologies, Miss Thorpe wrote that she thought that James Morland had been in low spirits when he left Bath for Oxford. He was the only man she could ever love, and she begged her dearest Catherine to clear up any misunderstanding. Captain Tilney had returned to his regiment, after disgracing himself by paying attention to another young lady. Isabella, herself, only wore purple now, in which she looked hideous, but it was the favourite colour of Catherine's dear brother. Even Catherine's kind heart could not promote this bare-faced attempt of Isabella's to catch again the fish she had thrown back, and she must have perceived the wisdom of giving no hint of the affair to General Tilney.

In an address to the Jane Austen Society, the novelist L. P. Hartley insisted that it was a mistake to believe that Jane Austen was, as a writer, incapable of tackling what he called 'the abyss'. He put forward the climax of *Northanger Abbey* as proof that her understanding of the baseness of the human heart was on a level with her sympathy for the heights to which it could rise.

Catherine had put from her mind the fantasies she had had about Northanger, which had become to her a pleasant house elegant and comfortable. The atmosphere had become even more agreeable at the departure of the General, with his uncertain temper, to London. On a Saturday night, Catherine and Eleanor were on their way to bed with the happy prospect of Henry returning on Monday from taking Sunday duty in his parish, when they heard the noise of a carriage driving to the door, and a loud peal on the house bell. At first surprised, Eleanor then assumed that her brother Frederick had arrived without warning as he sometimes did. She went downstairs to greet him, while Catherine retreated to her bedchamber, feeling some embarrassment at the idea of meeting the man responsible for breaking up her brother's engagement. Far worse was in store for her.

At night, during her early days at Northanger, Catherine had enjoyed tormenting herself at any noise that might be a sinister threat. Now she suddenly experienced a calamity as unexpected as it was unmerited, and which was signalled by a fumbling attempt to turn the handle of the door into her room. When, finally, the door opened, Eleanor was revealed, standing in the doorway with a look of such misery on her face that Catherine, panic-stricken, expected to hear bad news of Henry.

Eleanor reassured her, but with unabated distress. She had come, she said, on a deplorable errand. Her father had just returned, on recollecting that he had a long-standing engagement to take his family to visit Lord Longtown in Herefordshire. (General Tilney patronised his neighbours, but bent his knee to the peerage.) This was Saturday night, and the journey would be made on Monday. Catherine received this abrupt notice to quit with commendable good manners. The abyss began to yawn before her when Eleanor was obliged to tell her that the carriage was ordered to take her to the nearest posting-station at seven o'clock the following morning, regardless that it would be a Sunday, and that no servant would be sent to escort her.

This was a brutal rejection, and no one was more aware of its discourtesy and ill-breeding than

Eleanor, messenger of her father's order of expulsion. She could only hope that Catherine must have been conscious that her hostess' power in the household was without real authority. To an observer less courted than Catherine had been, it would have been obvious that General Tilney would have deserved top marks for Pride and Gluttony in an assessment of the Seven Deadly Sins. Later, it transpired that he was also strong on Avarice, but at the moment when he drove Catherine out of the Abbey, it was Anger, uncontrollable Anger, that had outdistanced the other Sins.

The complete rupture ordered by the General obliged Eleanor to refuse an invitation to Fullerton, and this was made even clearer to Catherine when Eleanor begged that a letter to assure her that Catherine had reached home should be sent under cover to her maid. To accept the subterfuge was too much even for Catherine's generous spirit, but Eleanor's distress, in the end, brought her to agree. It had also struck Eleanor that, having been so long from home, Catherine's funds might be low, and delicate inquiry found this to be the case. Without Eleanor's thoughtfulness, Catherine would have been expelled without the means to return to Fullerton. She struggled to leave a message of farewell to Henry, and it was in tears that she left Northanger where she had been so happily excited to arrive.

Catherine's youngest brother and sister were apt to be teased for expecting that any carriage passing by would be bringing home one of the family. So they enjoyed, for once, to be proved right, when the last of a series of post chaise deposited Catherine at the door of her father's house. The return of the eldest daughter was greeted with warmth and affec-

tion. The rather lame explanation for her expulsion
from Northanger was, of course, a subject of indignation, with Catherine struggling to assure her
parents of the guiltlessness of Eleanor and Henry in
the matter. Mrs Morland's advice, to cease to brood
on the General's brutal behaviour, was little consolation.

After three days, Mrs Morland began to feel that
her daughter was not only showing signs of undue
depression, but also symptoms of having been spoilt
by the luxuries of Northanger. The sensible mother
recalled 'a clever essay' on the subject of young girls
being spoilt from visits to houses grander than their
own. She thought it was in the first volume of *The
Mirror* (1779–1780) and went in search of that per-
iodical. Inevitably, Mrs Morland was delayed by the
household cares that spring up like weeds whenever
a housewife goes to look for anything. When she
managed to return to the room in which she had left
Catherine, she was astonished to find a visitor, a
young man she had never seen before. With extreme
bashfulness, Catherine introduced the stranger as 'Mr
Henry Tilney'.

While emphasising the good nature and tolerance
of Catherine's parents, Jane Austen obviously
enjoyed pointing out their blundering failure to
apprehend that their daughter's melancholy came
from a wounded heart, rather than discontent at the
simplicity of her home. Mr Tilney at once made an
apology for calling at a house where he felt he had
no right to expect a welcome, after the way Miss
Morland had been dismissed from his father's house.
Mrs Morland accepted the apologies with all the
warmth of her nature. She began, also, to suspect a
new aspect of her daughter's situation. When Mr

Tilney asked Catherine to show him the way to Mrs Allen's house, she hushed her next daughter, Sarah, who had officiously pointed out that the Squire's house could be seen from the window. Mrs Morland set aside the volume of *The Mirror* as not now needed.

It was just as well that Mrs Allen was of a dull disposition, only bestirring herself on matter of dress. Otherwise, she might have wondered at the abstracted state of mind into which her callers, particularly Catherine, seemed to have fallen. On the walk from the Parsonage, Henry had made Catherine blissfully happy by declaring his love. There was no impediment of coyness on Catherine's part. Henry had first been attracted to her by her obvious preference for himself. If this was rather a dreadful confession to make about her heroine, Jane Austen queried if it was such an unknown occurrence, even outside the world of novels.

Having settled that they were to be married, Henry could explain how he had arrived so precipitately at Fullerton. He had returned from his parish to Northanger to find his father in the towering rage of one who had made a spectacular fool of himself. The General commanded his son to cease from all thoughts of Miss Morland, and to accompany Eleanor into Herefordshire. Henry's indignation at his father's ejection of Catherine, together with his refusal to give up the idea of marrying her, further incensed his father. They had parted on the worst of terms.

To top up General Tilney's Anger, Pride and Avarice had come into play. It had been John Thorpe who had revealed that the General had fallen into a pit of his own digging. At Bath the fantasist Thorpe had painted such a glowing picture of the Morland family's prosperity that the General had been totally deceived. Wishing to increase the importance of his sister's betrothed, and planning to marry Catherine himself, Thorpe had halved Mr Morland's family, and doubled his property. He had further invented a handsome dôt for Catherine, and insisted that she was not only the protégée but the elected heiress of Mr Allen.

A chance meeting with John Thorpe in London dynamited the General's wish for Catherine as a daughter-in-law. Thorpe had failed to effect a reconciliation between his sister Isabella and James Morland, and had been rebuffed by Catherine on his own account. He worked a revenge by contradicting the rosy picture he had painted of the Morland's circumstances. He had, he regretted to tell the General, been misinformed. The Morlands were ill-reputed in their own neighbourhood, of small means, and wishing to better themselves by wealthy connexions, 'a forward bragging, scheming race'. When the General inquired as to the prospect of Mr Allen's estate, Thorpe assured him that he knew the young man on whom it must devolve. Breathing fire, General Tilney returned to Northanger. As he had only himself to blame, which he was not prepared to do, he relieved his feelings by casting out the innocent Catherine, guilty only of not being the heiress he had taken her to be.

Jane Austen wrote that she was well aware that the few remaining pages of this novel would warn her readers that the troubles of her heroine would be speedily resolved. Adroit though this process was, it did, unfortunately, mean the jettisoning of John Thorpe, the rattle. To the regret of many readers, he left the scene, still boasting. The mystery as to why a reasonably sensible young man, such as James Morland, could have tolerated such a cosmic liar as a friend can only be solved by reflecting on the appeal of exciting vulgarity for the otherwise decorous.

The Reverend Richard Morland and his wife were quite prepared to accept Henry Tilney as a husband for Catherine, his present means and prospects being adequate to support a wife. There was, however, the implacable figure of the General lowering on the horizon, and Catherine's parents required at least a formal acquiescence from Henry's father. With a final flourish, Jane Austen improved the General's temper by bestowing an excellent *parti* on his daughter Eleanor. The young man had unexpectedly inherited a Viscountcy and a fortune. Abiding, Jane Austen wrote, by the rule that no character who had not been linked with 'her fable' should be allowed to appear, it was the washing list left behind by the future Viscount's servant that Catherine hoped would reveal a truly 'horrid' story. His visit to Northanger had been in his days of poverty. Taking advantage of the General's admiration for the peerage, his daughter and son-in-law interceded on Henry's behalf.

Understanding that John Thorpe's malice was unfounded as had been his boasts, the General accepted that the Morlands were indeed neither needy nor disreputable. Having inquired privately about Mr Allen's estate, and learning it to be at the proprietor's disposal, the General gave Henry permission 'to be a fool if he liked it' and sent a page full of 'empty professions' to Catherine's parents. Regrettably, this letter was left to the reader's imagination, and so was the decision as to whether the novel 'recommended parental tyranny, or rewarded filial disobedience'.

6

Persuasion

'BARONET BLOOD'

Of the baronets who played important parts in Jane Austen's major novels, it might be said that they had little in common, except a habit of choosing wives of temperaments opposed to their own. Lady Middleton (*Sense and Sensibility*) was the chilly spouse of an exuberant husband. Sir Thomas Bertram (*Mansfield Park*) picked a beautiful young lady, who passed her life in a blameless torpor. Sir Walter Elliot (*Persuasion*) was fortunate in captivating a woman whose good sense protected him from the effects of his absurdly vain behaviour.

For seventeen years, Lady Elliot, née Elizabeth Stevenson, did her best to soften Sir Walter's exaggerated sense of his perfection in person and in station, which must have come close to making him a laughing stock among his neighbours. Dying, Lady Elliot had some comfort in the establishment of her friend, Lady Russell, in the village of Kellynch. She would do her best to protect the young Elliots from follies which might be committed by a widowed Sir Walter. Although solid rather than quick of mind,

Lady Russell was a woman of cultivation. Sir Walter, on the other hand, as the famous opening paragraph of *Persuasion* told the reader, 'was a man who, for his own amusement, never took up any book but the Baronetage'.

Jane Austen was sometimes heard to laugh when she had written a passage that particularly pleased her. The extract in 'the volume of honour', Sir Walter's favourite reading, which described the Elliot family, must have given her pleasure to compose. To the year of his wife's death, he had added the date and the month. Finally he had written in the name of his heir, his only son having been still-born. The honour of the Bloody Hand and the ownership of Kellynch Hall were destined to pass to William Walter Elliot, descendant of the second baronet, who had died a hundred years before.

Sir Walter had also added the date of his youngest daughter, Mary, to Charles Musgrove Esq. of Uppercross in the County of Somerset, the elder daughters, Elizabeth and Anne being unmarried. Elizabeth Elliot reigned as her widowed father's housekeeper with equal power, but more arrogance than Emma Woodhouse displayed in a similar situation at Hartfield. As has been seen, Eleanor Tilney had, in the same circumstances, no power even to protect her friend from expulsion by General Tilney from Northanger.

Still handsome at twenty-nine years old, Miss Elliot had begun to feel that it was time that she should be solicited by 'baronet blood'. Early in life she had decided, in conjunction with her father, that William Walter Elliot, the heir of Kellynch, would be the most suitable of husbands. A poor young man, reading for the bar, he had been patronised in

London, by Sir Walter, but a promised visit to Kellynch had not taken place. Elizabeth's hopes were still in suspense when she learnt that William Walter Elliot had found independence by marrying a rich woman of low origin. The breach was still unhealed when the novel opened, but convention required that Miss Elliot should be wearing black ribbons for the recently deceased wife of a cousin, who had not, to put it bluntly, come up to scratch.

One of Sir Walter's satisfactions was to contemplate with 'pity and contempt the endless creations [of baronetcies] of the last century'. Unfortunately, Jane Austen did not give the dates when Sir John Middleton and Sir Thomas Bertram received their honours, but the commercial origins of Lady Middleton's fortune, and the smallness of Lady Bertram's dowry, would surely have given Sir Walter a comfortable feeling of superiority.

It was the financial troubles of her father that set in motion the chain of happenings which was to rescue Anne Elliot from the lowly position in her family. If Elizabeth, as Miss Elliot, continued to open any ball of credit which 'a scanty neighbourhood afforded', Anne, her junior by two years, had faded into neglected spinsterhood. Only Lady Russell with her well-known good judgement, appreciated Anne's character and intelligence. When John Shepherd, Sir Walter's agent, found his employer helpless in any idea of retrenchment, he shifted the suggestion of unpopular economies on to Lady Russell, being confident that she would make the proposals he was determined should be adopted, while sparing him the odium of suggesting them. Shepherd was a most suitable name for this man of business, with his consummate skill of coaxing Sir Walter into the fold where he judged it fit for him to be.

The Law, as a profession, was a fruitful source for Jane Austen in her novels. The egregious Miss Bingley, in her efforts to sabotage Mr Darcy's growing interest in Elizabeth Bennet, pointed out that such a marriage would associate the proud Darcy with Elizabeth's Uncle Philip, the country attorney 'broad-faced stuffy . . . breathing port wine'. Mr Phillips' portrait might hang in the gallery at Pemberley, said Miss Bingley, as a pendant to that of Darcy's uncle, the Judge.

George Wickham surrendered his claim to a living in the gift of Fitzwilliam Darcy, and was given £3000, on which to support his proposed study of the Law (*Pride and Prejudice*). John Knightley, brother of Mr Knightley of Donwell Abbey, had a successful legal practice, even if he boasted that he dined with nobody. When Emma had failed, ludicrously, to make a match between Harriet Smith, and the Reverend Mr Elton, she wondered briefly if a Mr William Coxe might be a replacement. This idea was dismissed by Emma, William Coxe being unendurable, 'a pert young lawyer' (*Emma*).

If John Shepherd had ever been pert as a young lawyer, he had long ceased to be so at the date at which *Persuasion* opened. His ingratiation with Sir Walter and Miss Elliot had included his daughter Penelope Clay. She had returned, widowed, to her father, after an unprosperous marriage, which had left her with two children. Mrs Clay took every opportunity to accompany her father to Kellynch. She fawned assiduously on Elizabeth Elliot, and, though, she lacked the beauty which Sir Walter considered to be essential in an acceptable woman, he was flattered by her skill in pleasing.

In consultation with Anne, Lady Russell drew up a scheme of retrenchment, which should, after a period of years, free the estate from Sir Walter's debts. The suggested economies were received with horror by Sir Walter and Elizabeth. The former declared that he would rather quit Kellynch, than live there without the pomp that he considered his station required. This idea was pounced on by Mr Shepherd, who had been angling for such an arrangement. By leaving Kellynch immediate savings could be effected, without Sir Walter suffering the humiliation of being brought low in the eyes of his neighbours.

Before long a residence at Bath was accepted as a solution. Sir Walter had leanings towards London, but Mr Shepherd had good reason for not trusting his employer so far beyond his own influence. As has been said earlier, when Jane Austen was told that her father planned to resign his living and retire to Bath, she fainted. Anne Elliot did not go to the extreme of fainting, but she found little encouragement in Lady Russell's promise that her god-daughter should spend the summer months with her. Liking Bath herself, Lady Russell could not believe that it would not be equally good for everyone.

Meanwhile, Anne waited with resignation while Mr Shepherd manoeuvred Sir Walter towards accepting as ideal a possible tenant of whom Shepherd had heard rumours. Sir Walter had rejected, with horror, the idea of advertising, so Mr Shepherd's next approach was more circuitous. He suggested that the recent peace – the year was 1814 – would have turned ashore many naval officers, rich with prize money. He laughed obediently at Sir Walter's heavy jest that the tenancy of Kellynch would be a prize greater than any taken in war. He kept his head well below the parapet while Sir Walter inveighed against the Navy, as a profession that brought men of low birth into prominence, also ruining their looks by exposure to the weather. The first sign that Anne had a tender regard for the Navy here led her to assert herself with unusual force, in respect of the gratitude the country owed to its sailors.

Ever obsequious, Mrs Clay assured Sir Walter that only gentlemen of the titled and landed classes could hope to preserve, unimpaired, the beauty of their youth. Her earlier remark that naval officers were neat through their profession, and could be trusted to cherish Kellynch within and without, had not met with success. Sir Walter, like a nervous horse before an awkward fence, had shied away from the idea of a tenant having free use of his pleasure grounds. Mr Shepherd had supplied a soothing verbal plaster, but Mrs Clay obviously felt that Sir Walter needed an extra pabulum of flattery.

Having infiltrated the idea of a naval officer as a desirable tenant, Mr Shepherd now produced an excellent rabbit out of his hat. He had learnt that an Admiral Croft, wishing to retire to his native Somersetshire, was in search of a house to rent. Sir Walter listened with complacency to the suggestion, and even accepted the assurance that the Admiral was no more weather-beaten than might be expected after a life at sea. A surprisingly knowledgeable account of Admiral Croft's career, from the Trafalgar action onwards, was contributed by Anne.

Mr Shepherd's account of Mrs Croft's antecedents met with less success. She was, he said, the sister of a gentleman, a former neighbour, whose name escaped him. Once again, Anne supplied the needed information and the name of Wentworth. Sir Walter, putting his nose in the air, remarked frostily that Mr Wentworth, no man of property, had only held a local curacy. Neither was Mr Wentworth a connection of the Strafford family, and it was a wonder to Sir Walter how the names of the nobility had become so common.

There was a good reason for Sir Walter's attitude, though unknown to Mr Shepherd. Seven years earlier, Frederick Wentworth, brother of the Reverend Edward, had made his home at the latter's parsonage, while awaiting a naval appointment. Anne was then in the bloom of nineteen, Frederick a brilliant young officer with a promising career before him. They became betrothed, but Sir Walter regarded the match with cold contempt. Lady Russell, mistrusting Frederick Wentworth's light-hearted view of his future, felt the unwisdom to be too great, and the force of persuasion had induced the unhappy Anne to put an end to the engagement. Frederick Wentworth felt that Anne's lack of faith in his prospects was a sign of the weakness of her affection. He left the neighbourhood in what can only be called a huff, while Anne's beauty withered in the desolation of her spirits.

The prospect of Frederick's brother-in-law becoming the tenant of Kellynch was a test of Anne's fortitude, though this had been strengthened by seven years of burying her broken heart. She had had no difficulty in refusing a proposal from Charles Musgrove, son of a neighbouring squire with a fine property. Lady Russell would have urged acceptance, but Anne, taught prudence by one disastrous piece of persuasion, was in no mind to seek any more advice.

Charles Musgrove was then accepted by Mary, the youngest Miss Elliot. If Charles Musgrove thought that Mary might be a replica of Anne, he found that he had made a mistake, but both young Musgroves came to rely on Anne as a smoother of domestic troubles. Lacking the good looks that Elizabeth still had, and the delicate beauty Anne had once possessed, Mary soon took her place in Jane Austen's gallery of hypochondriacs.

The meeting between the baronet and his prospective tenant was carefully stage-managed by Mr Shepherd. He put Sir Walter on his best behaviour by intimating that the Admiral had heard reports of Sir Walter as a pattern of good breeding. Anne evaded the meeting, but afterwards learnt that her father considered the Admiral to be the best-looking sailor he had ever seen, presentable anywhere had the baronet's valet dressed the Admiral's hair. On the other hand, driving away from Kellynch, the Admiral gave it as his opinion to his wife that, though Sir Walter would never set the Thames on fire, there seemed no harm in him. Neither party being aware of the views of the other, the agreement that was to install the Crofts at Kellynch by Michaelmas could be duly completed.

Quailing at the 'possible heats of September in the white glare of Bath', Anne was almost glad to be rescued by the importunity of her sister Mary. The demand for her company was expressed with rank selfishness, Mary sometimes ailing, but suffering most when fancying herself neglected. At least Mary's appeal was less unattractive than Elizabeth Elliot's careless assertion that no one would want Anne in Bath. Between Kellynch Lodge and Uppercross Cottage, Anne was to be disposed of until Lady

Russell took her to Bath for the winter season. Satisfaction with this arrangement was almost destroyed for Lady Russell when she found that Mrs Clay was to accompany her dear Miss Elliot to Bath, as a helper in the move from Kellynch Hall.

Mrs Clay's toadying to Sir Walter had become so blatant, that Anne thought it right to draw Elizabeth's attention to the danger of the indigent widow becoming the second Lady Elliot. Anne was snubbed by Elizabeth, who had complete confidence that Mrs Clay's lowly opinion of herself would inhibit any aspiration towards 'baronet blood'. Besides Sir Walter, apparently never taught not to make personal remark, frequently criticised Mrs Clay's protruding tooth, clumsy wrist, and, in particular, her freckles. Miss Elliot did not, herself, feel as strongly as her father about freckles, but was convinced that this spotty pigmentation would be a stopper to Sir Walter in any possible romance.

As a rule, Jane Austen's technique required that each of her heroines should be, eventually, united to the man her heart had chosen. (The exception, Marianne Dashwood – *Sense and Sensibility* – had to be content with a second choice) But Jane Austen's appreciation of the married state was unclouded by illusion. When Anne Elliot arrived at her sister's house, she felt no regret that she had, herself, refused to marry Charles Musgrove. As the eldest son of the Great House of Uppercross, he had been given a farmhouse turned into an ornamental cottage. Four years, and two children, had brought their own scruffiness to what must have been, by today's standards a most desirable residence.

With a far nicer husband than her poor sense deserved, Mary ceaselessly bewailed her circumstances. She had little control over her children. Charles, her husband kept up his spirits by a sporting life, which caused him to be railed at for neglect of his suffering wife. Her father and mother-in-law, an old-fashioned country couple, were another source of discontent, both from the amount of room that they took up in their own carriage, and their meanness in not supplying their son with enough money to keep his own. Charles' sisters, Henrietta and Louisa, a cheerful couple, frequently caused Mary to grumble by their lack of respect towards herself as a baronet's daughter. Naturally, those at the Great House had an opposite set of grievances, but the closest contact was kept between the two houses, all plans and excursions being arranged in unison. Observing the annoyances this closeness caused to all parties, Anne could only do her best, as a general confidante, to smooth matters.

Anne, herself, had a far more serious embarrassment coming inescapably towards her. During a return call paid by Admiral and Mrs Croft, the latter said that she found it was Anne, rather than Mary, who had been an acquaintance of her brother. Had Anne heard that he was married? Anne suppressed her emotion, and then learnt that it was the Reverend Edward, rather than Captain Frederick, to whom Mrs Croft referred. Hardly had Anne recovered from the shock to her feelings than she heard the Admiral announce that a brother of his wife was immediately expected on a visit to Kellynch.

This news had an unexpected impact on the Great House at Uppercross. Mrs Musgrove, good-natured, but mentally limited, was visited by a sudden brainstorm. She recollected that her shiftless son Dick, sent to sea in desperation, had once served under a

Captain Wentworth. From her son's letters – death had promoted him to being 'poor Richard' – she found that it was indeed a Captain Wentworth who had been, briefly, a good influence on hopeless Dick Musgrove. (With her intimate knowledge of the Navy, Jane Austen knew that Dick Musgrove was the type of midshipman that every commander would strive to pass on, like a card at Old Maid.) Anne's fortitude was tested throughout the evening by speculation as to whether Mrs Croft's brother was indeed the Captain who had dealt kindly with 'poor Richard'. As this became more and more probable, Mr Musgrove senior, perhaps wishing to make up for his dead son's deficiencies, 'determined to welcome Captain Wentworth to all that was best and strongest in his cellars'.

Anne's meeting with Frederick Wentworth was delayed by an accident to little Charles Musgrove, on the day that dinner was to be eaten at the Great House. That the child was thought to be going on well did not prevent Mary, his mother, from going into hysterics, as was her custom in any crisis. At first the parents declared themselves unwilling to dine out. Then Charles thought he should gratify his father who wished him to meet the distinguished Captain. Anne was easily able to persuade Mary that she would look after little Charles, Mary declaring that her feelings as a mother would preclude her from usefulness.

When the delayed meeting with Frederick did take place, Anne suffered considerable pain. He had left Anne in scorn of what he thought of as her deplorable weakness of character, but she was then a young girl of delicate prettiness. Anne had tried to brace herself to face the fear that he might find her altered, and that he did so was conveyed crudely by her sister Mary. With a directness hardly to be excused by Mary's ignorance of Anne's previous engagement, Mary reported that Henrietta Musgrove had asked Captain Wentworth what he had thought of Miss Anne Elliot. He, unchivalrously, had replied that he would not have known her again.

The two Miss Musgroves, having a handsome newcomer for whom to compete, behaved with more generosity than Maria and Julia Bertram in an equivalent situation (*Mansfield Park*). Captain Wentworth showed towards both girls a cheerful friendliness, on the near side of gallantry. The only woman he treated with distant courtesy was Anne Elliot. They met frequently at the impromptu balls at the Great House, when Anne played the tunes to which Frederick danced with the younger girls. There was no breaking down the barrier between them. The past had inflicted 'a perpetual estrangement' on the present.

The first sign that this icy estrangement might be melting came when Captain Wentworth called at the cottage to find Anne, by herself, attending the convalescent little Charles. The next arrival was Charles Hayter, a clerk in Holy Orders, and a cousin of the Musgroves. He had been seen to be courting his cousin Henrietta, but her attention had been distracted by the attractive naval officer. Seeing the Captain as a rival, Charles Hayter resisted Wentworth's attempts to talk to him. At that moment the younger Musgrove, Walter, managed to get into the room, and began to persecute his aunt, who would not let him tease his sick brother. Climbing on her back, he was too strong for Anne to shake him off, and he refused the blandishments of Charles Hayter.

Suddenly, Anne found the child's arms detached from her neck, and realised that she had been released by Frederick Wentworth.

This kindness was painfully gratifying to Anne, and another incident, a few days later, convinced her that if Captain Wentworth had not forgiven her, he could not see her suffer without coming to her rescue. In the meantime, Charles Hayter, obviously chagrined by Henrietta's lack of interest in his prospect of becoming curate of Uppercross, remained at his parents' farm, Winthrop. Anne admired his strategy, though she had to listen to a dispute between her sister Mary and Charles Musgrove. Mary had an intense dislike for the Hayter family as beneath the notice of 'baronet blood'. Charles insisted that his cousin's prospects in the Church, and as the heir of Winthrop, were not to be despised.

It was in this mood that the whole party set out for a long autumn walk. The family's claustrophobic habits made it obligatory for the Miss Musgroves, originators of the scheme, not to start without calling on Mary. They called to say that they knew she would not care for as long a walk as they had in mind. Mary, disliking being supposed incapable of anything, refused to be left behind, as her sisters-in-law had obviously hoped. The unexpected return from a spoilt morning's shooting brought Mary's husband and Captain Wentworth to join the party, and Anne soon realised that the object of the walk was to reach the neighbourhood of Winthrop. Here there was a possibility of seeing the withdrawn Charles Hayter.

This manoeuvre only became clear to Mary Musgrove when she found herself on the hill above Winthrop, a plain house amid a huddle of farm buildings.

At her most socially offensive, Mary hastened to tell
Captain Wentworth it was disagreeable to have such
connections, and that she had seldom been in the
house. She was also obstinate in refusing to go down
and call on her husband's aunt. Charles insisted on
doing so and, after some urging from Louisa, Henrietta went with him. This left Louisa free to take
Captain Wentworth along a hedgerow – in this case
a path between two hedges – in search of a last
gleaning of hazelnuts.

When she was writing *Mansfield Park*, Jane Austen
is known to have inquired as to whether Northamptonshire was 'a country of hedgerows'.
Whatever the answer, she only mentioned a rough
hedgerow on the field at Mansfield Parsonage,
reserving the double hedgerow as a stratagem to
forward the plot of *Persuasion*. Resting on a sunny
bank, Anne could only listen with increasing
discomposure, while Louisa explained to Captain
Wentworth the significance of Henrietta's visit to
Winthrop.

It was only by her own persuasion, Louisa said,
that Henrietta had agreed to descend the hill and call
on her aunt, and, more importantly, reconcile herself
to her cousin Charles. Mary Musgrove's contempt
for the whole Hayter connection had nearly caused
Henrietta to change her mind. Having agreed that he
had observed Charles Hayter's partiality for Henrietta, manifested by unfriendliness towards himself as
a rival, the Captain might have added, he went on
to praise Louisa's firmness of mind. The author gave
him a speech comparing such a quality with the
soundness of hazelnut. Although the speech was sententious, to Anne, the hidden listener, it seemed an
advance in courtship.

Anne's pain was considerable, and it increased when Louisa told Captain Wentworth how much better pleased the Musgroves would have been if Anne had not refused Charles. Frederick inquired the date of this proposal, which, Anne knew, would have for him a significance unsuspected by Louisa. Anne was further distressed when Louisa went on to say she believed that Lady Russell had influenced Anne's refusal, considering Charles to be beneath Anne intellectually. Whatever his own feelings, Captain Wentworth might have felt some pity for the Musgroves. Anne's refusal of Charles had saddled the family for life with the perpetual grievances of the pettishly snobbish Mary.

Before the party started back for Uppercross, Charles Musgrove and Henrietta brought Charles Hayter to join them. Henrietta had relented towards her cousin, making over Captain Wentworth as the obvious partner for Louisa. Admiral and Mrs Croft were known to be driving in that part of the country, and there was speculation as to where they might overturn, the Admiral's driving being inferior to his seamanship.

Crossing a lane, the walkers coincided with the Croft's gig, and the offer of a lift was made to any lady who might be tired. The energetic Miss Musgroves refused, and so did Mary, incensed at the general invitation, and the indignity of sitting three in a one-horse shay. Anne had also refused, when Captain Wentworth vaulted over a hedge, and spoke to his sister. The invitation was insistently repeated, and, almost without her volition, Anne found herself helped into the gig by her former betrothed.

Once squeezed into the gig, Anne learnt that, while the Admiral was anxious that Frederick should make a quick choice from what was, to him, an indistinguishable pair of sisters, Mrs Croft had some reservations. While the talk continued, Mrs Croft found herself obliged to take charge of the reins, at intervals, averting disaster from running into a post, overturning in a rut, and, literally, falling foul of a dung-cart. The maxim that one should never, in any circumstances, interfere with the driver of a carriage, would seem to have been ignored by Mrs Croft, from the certainty that the Admiral would accept her guidance.

The disappearance of Captain Wentworth for two days came when Anne was faced with the prospect of a meeting between Frederick and Lady Russell, who was due to return to Kellynch Lodge, and to reclaim Anne. They did not like each other, he mistrusting Lady Russell's influence on Anne, and she suspicious of Frederick's headstrong brilliance. For the moment, there was a distraction when Captain Wentworth reappeared. He had been to seek his friend Captain Harville, settled for the winter at Lyme. It was admitted that Captain Harville was, to some extent, modelled on Jane Austen's brother Frank in his pursuits, though not in the distinguished career of Admiral of the Fleet, Sir Francis Austen GCB.

Captain Harville's retirement to Lyme was partly in the hope that the soft airs might improve health damaged by a wound two years before, and partly from economy. Unlike the childless Crofts, and the bachelor Frederick Wentworth, Captain Harville had the burden of a family, without, apparently, the prize money to make life easier.

Jane Austen's eulogy of Lyme, which included praise of the surrounding sights, Charmouth with its 'sweet retired bay', the landslip at Pinney, a garden of botanical delights, was much what Captain Wentworth must have described to the family at Uppercross. The young ladies were fired by his enthusiasm for the beauties he had seen there. Lyme was only twenty miles away, and Louisa, convinced that imposing her will was a prime virtue, overcame all opposition. The party set out, Anne and Mary travelling with the sisters in Mr Musgrove's coach, Charles driving Frederick in his curricle. At their chosen inn, there were apologies for the cul de sac of Lyme and the unfashionable season, but they were promised the best dinner the house could provide. Then they set off to visit the Harville family.

As Elizabeth Jenkins has written, in the year of *Persuasion*, 1814, the families of the novel would be surrounded by 'plain elegance, uncompromising good taste'. To Jane Austen, therefore, there was nothing to be considered remarkable in the buildings of Lyme itself. It would require no great leap of imagination to realise how delightful these unremarkable houses would look to the house hunters of today. Welcoming as the Harvilles were, they almost took it amiss that Captain Wentworth had not assumed that he and five friends would dine with them. An astounding price would certainly be asked for the house which Captain Harville had rented, though to Anne Elliot the rooms were so small that 'none but those who invite from the heart could think of accommodating such a numerous party.'

Besides the sensible Captain Harville, his slightly less polished wife and a number of children, the house also sheltered a Captain Benwick. This officer was regarded with pitying interest by the ladies of the Uppercross party. He had been engaged to Captain

Harville's sister, Fanny, who had died while he was at sea, and just come into possession of the prize-money for which their marriage had waited. Much cast down by his loss, Captain Benwick was settled with the dead Fanny's family, but he lacked the resources of carpentry, and the crocheting of a fishing net, which Captain Harville had in common with Frank Austen.

Captain Benwick, on the other hand, was fond of reading with a strong taste for poetry, as Anne discovered when he came with Captain Harville to spend an evening at the inn, with the party from Uppercross. Struggling with a feeling of lowness at thinking that she might have married into such a warm-hearted circle, Anne did her best for Captain Benwick, although after showing his heart-broken state by quotations from Sir Walter Scott and Lord Byron, there seemed little hope of raising his spirits. Anne recommended reading more prose and less poetry, but, grateful for her attention, Captain Benwick showed signs of wishing to nurse his grief. Anne, with the objectivity that saved her character from insipidity, could only reflect that, 'like many other great moralists and preachers, she had been eloquent on a point in which her own conduct would ill bear examination.'

That Captain Wentworth had kept more interest in Anne than he probably admitted to himself, became clear during a morning walk at Lyme, when he, the Miss Musgroves and Anne were climbing up the steps from the beach. The sea wind had brought back a bloom to Anne's pretty features, and a stranger, met on the steps, stood back in obvious, if polite, admiration. Frederick gave Anne a glance which might have belonged to their lost past, admitting that her glowing face reminded him of how she had once looked. This unknown gentleman happened to meet Anne again in the passage of the inn, a collision being narrowly avoided. His apology was well-mannered, and he managed to convey how much he admired her looks. This boost to the esteem of a maiden aunt, and family victim, led Anne to wish to know who the stranger might be.

Her wish was gratified, immediately and surprisingly. Frederick, who had remarked the stranger's interest in Anne, gave her a slightly conspiratorial glance, and asked a waiter if he knew the departing gentleman's name. Astoundingly, the name was 'Elliot', and its bearer said to be the heir of a baronetcy. This, it became clear, was William Walter Elliot, a distant cousin, but heir presumptive to Sir Walter. Inept as usual, Mary began to regret that there had been no meeting. She ignored Anne's hints that Mr Elliot was estranged from the head of the family. Anne, herself, had suppressed her second meeting with Mr Elliot, knowing Mary's resentment of attention to anyone but Mrs Charles Musgrove.

The final walk along The Cobb, when Captain Benwick quoted Byron's lines about 'dark blue seas' to Anne, ended with a drama, unique in its violence among Jane Austen's novels. Brimming with vitality, Louisa loved to be jumped down from styles into the hands of Captain Wentworth. She now insisted that he should catch her as she jumped from a flight of steps in the wall of The Cobb. Although Wentworth protested that the pavement was too hard, Louisa ran up the step to have the pleasure of a second leap. She jumped, but just missed the young man's hands, and knocked herself out cold on the paving stones below. (When Alfred, Lord Tennyson, visited Lyme, he brushed aside references to Monmouth's landing. Preferring fiction to history, he demanded, where were the steps from which Louisa Musgrove fell?)

A dashing and successful naval commander, Captain Wentworth found himself in a state of shock, holding a senseless, possibly dead, Louisa in his arms. Sensibility added to the list of casualties. Henrietta fainted into Anne's arms, while Mary immobilised her husband by clinging to him in hysterics. When Frederick appealed for help, the only practical assistance came from Anne. She gave advice as to elementary first aid, and produced that panacea of the period, smelling salts.

It was Anne who sent Captain Benwick for a surgeon, and dealt with every aspect of the chaotic situation, which included trying to assuage Captain Wentworth's feelings of guilt and horror at the result of letting Louisa have her wilful way. The Harvilles insisted that Louisa, who had once opened her eyes, should be carried in and laid on Mrs Harville's bed. Meanwhile, some measure of self-control was achieved by Henrietta and Mary, having done their best to hinder Anne's command of the situation.

Captain Wentworth's thankfulness was intense, when the surgeon made a hopeful prognosis of Louisa's injury. Anne, for her part, could not help herself from wondering if there might not be reasonable limits to firmness of character, and if this idea might not occur to Frederick. These reflections came to her when, contrary to her wildest dreams, she found herself in a chaise and four on the road to Uppercross, with Captain Wentworth sitting between Henrietta and the woman against whom he thought he had closed his heart. This arrangement came about by the disruption of a sensible plan, by which Anne, at Frederick's request, should stay to nurse Louisa in the Harvilles' house.

Mary, ever anxious to keep the centre of the stage, had insisted that, as Louisa was her sister, she had the right to stay, though her uselessness was apparent to all. Charles was determined not to leave Louisa in her unconscious state, and Mary would certainly not go home without him. Anne had to capitulate, not the least of her regrets being that Captain Wentworth showed, only too clearly, his disappointment at leaving Louisa to what could only be a pretence at nursing from the self-important and incompetent Mary. Anne's consolation was that he still relied on her as he had throughout the crisis. He had overcome his attack of nervous shock, and returned to be the decisive man of action.

Still in control of the rather helpless Musgroves, Anne managed to persuade the Uppercross party, parents, sister and old family nurse, to Lyme, while she herself returned to Kellynch Lodge and the sympathies of Lady Russell. The only embarrassment was the necessity to explain that Captain Wentworth had been a frequent visitor to the Musgroves. Lady Russell's opinion of the Captain obviously did not improve when Anne explained that he was likely to marry Louisa Musgrove. This victim of her own obstinacy was recovering, but still detained at Lyme.

The Musgroves returned to Uppercross for the Christmas holidays, leaving the convalescent Louisa to the care of the Harvilles, but bringing the Harville children with them. Captain Wentworth, to avoid upsetting Louisa's nerves, had gone to visit his brother the Reverend Edward, but Captain Benwick remained at Lyme. Charles Musgrove was determined that he was likely to appear at Kellynch in pursuit of Anne, which Mary, in her jealousy, denied. A call at Uppercross, where the Christmas holidays were in full blast, resolved Lady Russell never to risk such a riot again. Her taste was for the winter pleasures of Bath, notwithstanding rain and the raucous city noises. She deposited Anne at Sir Walter's rented house in Camden Place. Anne herself could only hope that her incarceration would not be indefinite.

Anne's welcome from her family was warmer than previous experience had led her to expect. Elizabeth boasted of the handsome drawing-room in their hired house, and of the society which courted Sir Walter and Miss Elliot. There was also the saga of the reconciliation of the next heir, that Mr Elliot with whom Anne had had a brief meeting at Lyme. Her sister and father paid little attention, but when, at ten o'clock, there was a ring at the door, and Mr Elliot was announced, he was clearly delighted to see Anne again.

Sir Walter formally presented Mr Elliot to 'his youngest daughter', having sunk Mary for the moment, and had Elizabeth been less confident of her superior attraction she might have smelt danger at the vivacity with which Mr Elliot, now her destined prey, had claimed acquaintance with her sister. He took a sympathetic interest in Anne's account of the accident at Lyme. She found him likely to be an alleviation in the oppressive dullness of Bath society.

One agent of reconciliation between Sir Walter and his heir had been a Colonel Wallis. (Jane Austen's Colonels with the exception of Colonel Forster – *Pride and Prejudice* – seemed to have had a good deal of time on their hands.) It was Colonel Wallis who explained away Mr Elliot's marriage to a woman of low degree. The lady, rich and handsome, had been much in love with Mr Elliot, which to Sir Walter was an excuse for inequality of birth. Elizabeth might have continued to feel slighted, but for Mrs Clay's hints that Mr Elliot looked up to Sir Walter as to a father, or a prospective father-in-law.

Although continuing to find Mr Elliot the most agreeable of her acquaintances in Bath, Anne had reservations about what she learnt to be his earlier habits. Jane Austen sent Catherine Morland (*Northanger Abbey*) home by post chaise on a Sunday, without accusing General Tilney of the additional offence of forcing his rudely ejected guest into Sabbath-breaking. Anne Elliot, on the other hand, was represented as disapproving of the 'Sunday travelling', which seemed to been frequent in Mr Elliot's past life. Even more was she unsympathetic to his regard for rank, which was brought to Anne's notice by the arrival in Bath of the Dowager Viscountess Dalrymple, and her daughter, the Honourable Miss Carteret.

Having become inured by the high opinion of their own position held by her family, Anne was staggered by the panic into which the arrival of these cousins – presumably at some distance – threw Sir Walter and his eldest daughter. A lack of letters of condolence had caused the acquaintance to lapse, but the idea of Bath society resting in ignorance of the Elliots' kinship with Lady Dalrymple and Miss Carteret was more than Sir Walter could tolerate. Mr Elliot supported the wish to claim relationship, and this was the cause of disagreement between Anne and her cousin.

Mr Elliot put forward his idea that good company was always worth seeking. To this Anne replied that her idea of good company was that of 'clever, well-informed people, who have a great deal of conversation.' Her model can only have been Captain Wentworth, the one bright star in her narrow circle. Mr Elliot assured her that this was not 'good company', but, rather, the best. He defended his opinion by implying that association with noble kinswomen might distract Sir Walter from his increasing attentions to Mrs Clay. This scheming widow had been retained in Bath by Elizabeth Elliot, who found such a toady far more congenial than her sister Anne.

Sir Walter showed his revised opinion of Mrs Clay's looks when he complimented Anne on her improved appearance. He assumed that she had been using Gowland, identified by Doctor Chapman as an expensive lotion for the skin, price 8/6. Gowland, according to Sir Walter, had quite carried away Mrs Clay's freckles. He had also urged Mrs Clay to continue her visits, at least until her 'fine mind' had been gratified by the sight of the beautiful Mrs Wallis, daily awaiting her confinement. Mrs Clay lost no opportunity for assuring Elizabeth of Mr Elliot's intentions of becoming Sir Walter's son-in-law.

Lady Russell, on the other hand, suspected that Mr Elliot was, in reality, courting Anne. Questioned on the subject, Anne failed to respond to Lady Russell's tempting picture of herself installed in Kellynch as a happier Lady Elliot than her mother had been. Anne was also unable to follow Lady Russell in her willingness to see Lady Dalrymple and Miss Carteret as desirable acquaintances. Lady Dalrymple had nothing more to recommend her than a vacuous civility, while her daughter could only be called a lump, unacceptable to Sir Walter and Miss Elliot had she been of lowlier station. Sir Walter's letter of explanation, and apology for past neglect, was accepted in a brief scrawl from Lady Dalrymple, 'The toils of the business were over, the sweets began.'

While her father and sister were fawning on the Dalrymples, in the style that Mrs Clay had perfected towards themselves, Anne had gone in search of a former school-fellow. Sent to school soon after the death of her mother, Anne had been comforted and befriended by an older Miss Hamilton. She now learnt that her friend, as the widowed Mrs Smith, was living in straitened circumstances in unsalubrious West Gate Buildings. Her late husband's financial carelessness had left her with little means to struggle with a rheumatic complaint, but Anne found Mrs Smith supporting her poverty and helplessness with admirable fortitude.

Anne's visits to Mrs Smith linked her to a circle whose gossip, by way of her friend, shed new light on possible marriages among the Elliot family. In the meantime, however, a letter from Mary Musgrove brought Anne a piece of news which shattered the careful guard she had set about her heart, and filled it with 'joy, senseless joy'. The first part of Mary's letter was a doleful wail. There was a bad throat about, and Anne must know that Mary's sore throats were worse than anyone else's. (Addressing the Jane Austen Society, L. P. Hartley expressed sympathy with Mary Musgrove. His own sore throats were, he was convinced, always worse than anyone else's.)

The Crofts did not improve as neighbours, Mary wrote, in that they were going to Bath and had not offered to take messages. This complaint was suddenly reversed, when the Crofts did, after all, offer to take letters to Mary's family. In consequence, she was able to write at fuller length, without thought of the postal charges which were, at that date, a serious expense. The news she had to tell was so extraordinary in its improbability, that Anne's 'senseless joy' was mingled with wild astonishment.

Louisa, before her accident the most bouncing of girls, had returned to Uppercross engaged to the poetry-loving Captain Benwick. Mary could not resist a sisterly jab at the absurdity of her husband's insistence that Captain Benwick was in love with Anne. Although she had no wish to dispute the matter, Anne was privately convinced that Captain Benwick's widowed heart was an affectionate one. He could grieve, but he must love. She could only rejoice that Louisa's convalescence had provided him with an object. Benwick might have to widen Louisa's mind with readings from Scott and Byron, but, under the tutelage of Captain Wentworth, she already had a fine enthusiasm for the Navy.

And while the stones of Winchester and Milsom
                                    Street remain,
Glory, love and honour, unto England's Jane.
                        Rudyard Kipling, *The Janeites*

It was in Milsom Street that the tendrils of Anne's hopes began increasingly to unfurl. She found Admiral Croft before a shop window, studying the picture of a ship, and marvelling at her unseaworthiness. Mrs Croft was immobilised by a blistered heel, and feeling lost without a woman's hand in his elbow, the Admiral gave Anne his arm. He had, he said, a piece of news for her, but took his time in telling it, comments on naval friends and foes interrupting his narration. Finally, the Admiral announced Captain Benwick's engagement to Louisa, and, by some verbal manoeuvering, Anne was able to assure herself that in a letter to Mrs Croft, Frederick showed no signs of hurt feelings. Furthermore the Admiral, a hand over fist match-maker, asked Anne if she did not think his brother-in-law should come to Bath, where he would have a garden of girls from whom to choose a wife.

With a mind made up, more than he perhaps realised, Captain Wentworth arrived in Bath the very next day. Anne saw him in the street from a shop in which she was waiting for Elizabeth to negotiate a lift from Lady Dalrymple. It was indeed raining, but Elizabeth's object was to demonstrate publicly, her intimacy with her aristocratic cousins. Mr Elliot was, as ever, in attendance, and having arranged for Lady Dalrymple to take up Elizabeth and Mrs Clay, he returned to escort Anne. He returned to find Anne, for once the least embarrassed, in conversation with Captain Wentworth. Like two dogs the hackles of the gentlemen rose, and after Anne had been walked off by her cousin, Captain Wentworth heard comments which indicated Mr Elliot's courtship was a subject for Bath gossip.

This animated his attitude towards Anne, who now had to explain Louisa's engagement to Lady Russell. This second example of Louisa being preferred to Anne can only have increased Lady Russell's distrust of the Navy, for it freed Captain Wentworth to be once again a threat to Anne's future.

To Anne the tantalising knowledge that Frederick was in Bath, but unwelcome to her chilly family, was only alleviated by the hope of meeting him at a concert. Love of music might well give them an opportunity to come to an understanding. She visited Mrs Smith to excuse herself from a semi-engagement, and was baffled and embarrassed by

Mrs Smith's hints that she suspected Anne's visits might soon come to an end.

At the concert, Anne, so often neglected, found herself in the position of having two strings to her bow. Captain Wentworth walked into the Assembly Rooms, when the Elliots were waiting the arrival of the Dalrymples. There was time for Anne and Frederick to shorten the lines of misunderstanding that had kept them apart for so many years. Even Sir Walter and Miss Elliot acknowledged the acquaintance of the distinguished officer who they had spurned as a penniless adventurer. Verbal skirmishing on the subject of Louisa's engagement to Captain Benwick, led Frederick to declare that he considered Louisa inferior to the deceased Fanny Harville, and to add that a man should not so easily forget such a superior being. This statement of policy filled Anne with a gladness that made it easier to bear the obsequious behaviour of her father and sister towards their noble cousins.

Mr Elliot certainly scented a rival, and attracted Anne's interest by claiming to have been long familiar with the name of Anne Elliot, but refusing, as it were, to name his source. He even breathed a hint that he hoped the name might never be changed. With this knight's move by Mr Elliot on the chessboard of courtship, Anne was certainly intrigued, but Captain Wentworth was far more on her mind, and she edged her way to the end of the bench, making herself more accessible. Inconveniently, when success was almost in sight, Mr Elliot asked her for a translation of the Italian love song, next to be sung, Miss Carteret wishing to know. Good manners required Anne to give a rendering, though she had claimed to be a poor Italian scholar. Mr Elliot had agreed, adding that she obviously knew nothing of the matter, merely rendering inverted Italian lines into elegant English. By these exchanges Captain Wentworth was also alerted to a rival, and retreated in a jealous pique. Anne could only scheme as to how to convey her unwavering fidelity to its object.

On the morning after the concert, Anne hurried to pay her postponed visit to Mrs Smith, being particularly anxious to be out at the hour of Mr Elliot's usual call. She regarded his attentions as doing incalculable harm to her newly established relationship with Frederick. Anne had been aware that Mrs Smith suspected a love-affair in the background, but on this morning she found Mrs Smith had the conviction that Anne had spent the concert in the company of the person she felt to be the most agreeable in the world.

Anne was baffled as to how Mrs Smith, even with an excellent intelligence system could have found out that she, Anne, was attached to Captain Wentworth. They talked at cross purposes, until it became clear that Mrs Smith was expecting the announcement of Anne's engagement to Mr Elliot, known to Mrs Smith in her days of prosperity, but now, it seemed, estranged from her.

With the help of letters preserved, fortunately, by Mrs Smith, Anne learnt how sound her instinct to suspect a flaw in Mr Elliot's nature had been. The story unrolled of a poor young William Walter Elliot, continually helped by his friend Smith, and accepted as a member of the family by Smith's young wife. At this period Mr Elliot wrote disrespectfully of Sir Walter and Elizabeth. Should he inherit Kellynch, his first visit would be with an auctioneer to learn how to turn the house into ready money. Anne then learnt that with Mr Elliot's marriage, the relationship between him and the Smiths had been reversed. With the money that came with his wife, daughter of a grazier and granddaughter of a butcher, he encouraged Smith's natural extravagance, and refused help when Smith got into difficulties.

After her husband's death, Mrs Smith found that Mr Elliot's heart had grown even colder. He refused to act as executor, and to assist Mrs Smith in disentangling her claims to one of those West Indian estates, which, as in *Mansfield Park*, needed energetic action. When Anne had grasped the details of Mr Elliot's career, and learnt of his unkindness towards his wife, she had still a protest to make. Allowing that he had been courting her, he had, however, reconciled himself to her family before he had known her identity.

This puzzle was cleared up by Mrs Smith's friend, Nurse Rooke. Middle life and riches had made Mr Elliot desirous of the honours he had spurned as a poor young man. To secure his future, it was important to prevent Sir Walter from marrying again. Watchfulness required him to be on the spot, and he was prepared to take the first steps. Colonel Wallis was the intermediary through whom the reconciliation took place. Mrs Wallis had passed on her husband's confidences to Nurse Rooke, her midwife, a woman of robust sense and wit. Mrs Wallis declared that, when Anne married Mr Elliot, the settlements should include the stipulation that Sir Walter must not marry Mrs Clay. Nurse Rooke, professionally a friend of matrimony as a prelude to confinements, pointed out that this would not prevent Sir Walter from marrying anyone else. Mrs Smith suspected that the midwife had visions of delivering an infant of Sir Walter's second marriage.

To explain to Lady Russell the villainy of her favoured Mr Elliot as a husband for Anne, was a matter of urgency. Anne only lingered to avoid walking with Mrs Clay, Mr Elliot himself being known to be out of town for the day. To her best love, which Elizabeth asked Anne to give Lady Russell, she added the rider that she had thought Lady Russell's dress had been hideous at a recent party. Sir Walter said that he would call, but only leave his card, as it was unfair to visit ageing women in the morning, particularly if they did not wear rouge.

These civil messages were interrupted by the arrival of Mr and Mrs Charles Musgrove. The Musgrove family caravan had put up at the White Hart, Mrs Musgrove bringing Captain Harville as her guest, and Henrietta, to buy wedding clothes for Louisa and herself. Anne was delighted to be claimed as one of the Musgrove party, but Elizabeth was appalled at the idea that she might be obliged to ask that party to dinner. The descent from the style of entertaining at Kellynch would be too much to bear, and Elizabeth convinced herself that a small, but elegant, evening party would be more appreciated. Having decided the matter, Elizabeth and her father called at the White Hart, with a handful of cards, 'Miss Elliot At Home', one of which was offered to Captain Wentworth.

In the course of the morning, an incident caused Anne disquiet in her efforts to convince Captain Wentworth that she had no interest in her cousin. Mary Musgrove, at a window of the White Hart, declared that under the colonnade she had had a sight of Mrs Clay. What was even more interesting to

Mary was to recognise that Mrs Clay was in conversation with Mr Elliot. Thoughtlessly, Anne declared this to be impossible. Mr Elliot, she knew, was absent from Bath for the day. Anne hoped, however, to display detachment by admitting it to be Mr Elliot, but adding that she had paid little real heed to his plans.

The conjunction of Mr Elliot, known to be determined to keep his position as Sir Walter's heir, and Mrs Clay, suspected by Anne of doing her best to thwart these plans, was so surprising, that Anne later mentioned to Mrs Clay that she had been seen in Mr Elliot's company. Although there was some degree of guilt in Mrs Clay's face, Anne put this down to having had to listen to a demand that she should restrict her designs on Sir Walter. Mrs Clay dismissed the meeting as mere chance, leaving her with no notion as to why Mr Elliot should be still in Bath. All she could answer for was that he wished to arrive at the earliest moment at his cousin Elizabeth's card-party. This was an indication, unsuspected by Anne, that more than one can play a double game.

The following morning, Anne arrived at the White Hart to find Captain Harville, Captain Wentworth and Mrs Croft already present. Mrs Croft was adding her good sense to the kindly vapourings of Mrs Musgrove, on the subject of Henrietta's engagement, which brighter prospects in the Church for Charles Hayter had made possible. Both ladies were, at least, in agreement that any modest start in married life was better than a long engagement. Anne, trembling between happiness and misery, could only feel more shaken, when Frederick gave her a look which seemed to apply the talk of the evils of a long engagement to themselves.

Realising that Captain Harville wished to speak to her, Anne moved into the window where he stood, and found herself nearer the table at which Captain Wentworth was writing a letter. Captain Harville's purpose was to show Anne a miniature of Captain Benwick, which had been painted for the deceased Fanny Harville. Captain Wentworth's letter was to arrange that the picture should now be framed for Louisa Musgrove. As Fanny's brother, Captain Harville felt that she would not have forgotten him so soon. It was only when Anne had almost convinced Captain Harville that women could love longer when life or hope was gone that she realised how close was the table where Captain Wentworth sat writing.

It was now that the gradual removal of the obstacles that had separated Anne and Frederick gathered speed. Having left the room without a glance at Anne, Frederick returned. He had forgotten his gloves for a very good purpose. Obviously agitated, he placed a letter before Anne, and again left the room. Anne found the letter to be entirely satisfactory. It was a declaration of a love that had never failed in constancy, in spite of his foolish efforts to give his heart elsewhere. If Anne had nearly broken his heart by her original dismissal, she had mended it by her overheard dissertation on the longer lasting constancy of women, living, as they did, home-bound lives.

Captain Wentworth had struck an attitude by asking for one word from Anne, which was to decide him if he was to enter her father's house that evening, or never appear there again. To settle the matter, and to be certain that a message reached Frederick, Anne asked Mrs Musgrove to be sure that the two Captains realised that they were both invited to Elizabeth's party. Mrs Musgrove, in her habitual state of woolly-mindedness, was aware that Captain Harville knew he was invited, and added that, probably, Captain Wentworth was aware of his invitation.

Anne's experience of the last few months had strengthened her character, and she ceased to flinch at a possible set-back. She would have a means of sending a message by Captain Harville should Frederick not arrive at the party. The joyful shock of her letter had, however, made her discomposure so obvious, that the Musgroves tried to persuade her to go home in a chair, the rickshaw of Bath. Anne had to struggle to insist on walking, confident that Frederick would be waiting for her. She was right, and when Charles Musgrove, her escort, found that Captain Wentworth had joined them, he left the pair together, while he kept an engagement with a gunsmith. The love that had been born, and seemed to die, at Kellynch was brought back to life in Union Street, Bath.

Frederick admitted that he had been brought to his senses when he realised that the Harvilles considered him engaged to Louisa. Relief at her recovery was shattered by the knowledge that honour would oblige him to marry her. No sooner did he find himself released by her engagement to Captain Benwick, and able to pursue Anne to Bath, than he found Mr Elliot, impeccably eligible, regarded as likely to become engaged to Anne. These explanations only added to Anne's happiness. Frederick had left Lyme to visit his brother Edward, who had inquired if he, Frederick, had found Anne to be altered, 'little suspecting that to my eyes you could never alter'. This loving tribute obliterated the ungallant speech of not knowing her again, obligingly reported by Mary only three months before.

Sir Walter, who, in the past, had complained of the name Wentworth not, in this case, belonging to the Strafford family, was now glad to have such a fine-sounding patronymic to enter into the baronetage as a son-in-law, sweetened by the £25000 that his gallant career had brought Captain Wentworth. Mary Musgrove was also pleased, because her own sister would be richer than the sisters of her husband.

Elizabeth on the other hand, took little interest in Anne's marriage, and was herself faced with two humiliations. Mr Elliot, realising that his cover was blown, left Bath, to be followed by Mrs Clay. She was next heard of established under Mr Elliot's protection in London. His efforts to distract her from her designs on Sir Walter had been only too successful, but Jane Austen speculated that Mrs Clay might manipulate her lover so cunningly that he would find himself making Penelope Clay the wife of Sir William Elliot. Abandoned by their own toadies, Sir Walter and Miss Elliot were presumably reduced to 'the stupidity of private parties' as the forlorn sycophants of the Dalrymples.

On his marriage, Captain Wentworth not only provided Anne with a very pretty landaulette, but undertook to straighten out the business affairs of Mrs Smith. Lady Russell had no choice but to rejoice in Anne's happiness, and Captain Wentworth promised to endeavour to forgive Lady Russell for her interference. Anne's sufferings through the winter before she was reunited to Frederick had developed in her qualities of confidence and practicality. If she did not provide the sort of ballast that Mrs Croft gave to the Admiral, it would be likely that her persuadable temper might be a steadying influence on the impetuous streak in Captain Wentworth's nature.

Northanger Abbey and *Persuasion* were published in 1818, about six months after Jane Austen had been laid to rest under the stones of Winchester Cathedral. The slab on her grave is inscribed with affectionate admiration for her qualities and talents, but without mentioning her achievements as a novelist. This delicacy, has not, however, hindered the ever-increasing and worldwide devotion for the glorious army of characters which was her gift to English language and literature.

Index

Index